PENGUIN SHAKESPEARE

Founding Editor: T. J. B. Spencer
General Editor: Stanley Wells
Supervisory Editors: Paul Edmondson, Stanley Wells

T. J. B. SPENCER, sometime Director of the Shakespeare Institute of the University of Birmingham, was the founding editor of the New Penguin Shakespeare, for which he edited both *Romeo and Juliet* and *Hamlet*.

STANLEY WELLS is Emeritus Professor of the University of Birmingham and Chairman of the Shakespeare Birthplace Trust. He is general editor of the Oxford Shakespeare and his books include *Shakespeare: The Poet and His Plays*, *Shakespeare: For All Time*, *Looking for Sex in Shakespeare* and (with Paul Edmondson) *Shakespeare's Sonnets*.

HELEN HACKETT is a Reader in English Literature at University College London. Her publications include *Virgin Mother, Maiden Queen: Elizabeth I and the Cult of the Virgin Mary*, *Writers and Their Work: 'A Midsummer Night's Dream'* and *Women and Romance Fiction in the English Renaissance*.

William Shakespeare

A MIDSUMMER
NIGHT'S DREAM

Edited with a Commentary by Stanley Wells
Introduced by Helen Hackett

PENGUIN BOOKS

PENGUIN BOOKS

Published by the Penguin Group
Penguin Books Ltd, 80 Strand, London WC2R ORL, England
Penguin Group (USA) Inc., 375 Hudson Street, New York, New York 10014, USA
Penguin Group (Canada), 10 Alcorn Avenue, Toronto, Ontario, Canada M4V 3B2
(a division of Pearson Penguin Canada Inc.)
Penguin Ireland, 25 St Stephen's Green, Dublin 2, Ireland (a division of Penguin Books Ltd)
Penguin Group (Australia), 250 Camberwell Road, Camberwell, Victoria 3124, Australia
(a division of Pearson Australia Group Pty Ltd)
Penguin Books India Pvt Ltd, 11 Community Centre, Panchsheel Park, New Delhi – 110 017, India
Penguin Group (NZ), cnr Airborne and Rosedale Roads, Albany, Auckland 1310, New Zealand
(a division of Pearson New Zealand Ltd)
Penguin Books (South Africa) (Pty) Ltd, 24 Sturdee Avenue, Rosebank 2196, South Africa

Penguin Books Ltd, Registered Offices: 80 Strand, London WC2R ORL, England

www.penguin.com

This edition first published in Penguin Books 1967
Reissued in the Penguin Shakespeare series 2005

014

This edition copyright © Penguin Books, 1967
Account of the Text and Commentary copyright © Stanley Wells, 1967
General Introduction and Chronology copyright © Stanley Wells, 2005
Introduction, The Play in Performance and Further Reading copyright © Helen Hackett, 2005

All rights reserved

The moral right of the editors has been asserted

Set in 11.5/12.5 PostScript Monotype Fournier
Typeset by Palimpsest Book Production Limited, Polmont, Stirlingshire
Printed in England by Clays Ltd, St Ives plc

ISBN-13: 978–0–141–01260–5

www.greenpenguin.co.uk

Contents

General Introduction

Every play by Shakespeare is unique. This is part of his greatness. A restless and indefatigable experimenter, he moved with a rare amalgamation of artistic integrity and dedicated professionalism from one kind of drama to another. Never shackled by convention, he offered his actors the alternation between serious and comic modes from play to play, and often also within the plays themselves, that the repertory system within which he worked demanded, and which provided an invaluable stimulus to his imagination. Introductions to individual works in this series attempt to define their individuality. But there are common factors that underpin Shakespeare's career.

Nothing in his heredity offers clues to the origins of his genius. His upbringing in Stratford-upon-Avon, where he was born in 1564, was unexceptional. His mother, born Mary Arden, came from a prosperous farming family. Her father chose her as his executor over her eight sisters and his four stepchildren when she was only in her late teens, which suggests that she was of more than average practical ability. Her husband John, a glover, apparently unable to write, was nevertheless a capable businessman and loyal townsfellow, who seems to have fallen on relatively hard times in later life. He would have been brought up as a Catholic, and may have retained

Catholic sympathies, but his son subscribed publicly to Anglicanism throughout his life.

The most important formative influence on Shakespeare was his school. As the son of an alderman who became bailiff (or mayor) in 1568, he had the right to attend the town's grammar school. Here he would have received an education grounded in classical rhetoric and oratory, studying authors such as Ovid, Cicero and Quintilian, and would have been required to read, speak, write and even think in Latin from his early years. This classical education permeates Shakespeare's work from the beginning to the end of his career. It is apparent in the self-conscious classicism of plays of the early 1590s such as the tragedy of *Titus Andronicus*, *The Comedy of Errors*, and the narrative poems *Venus and Adonis* (1592–3) and *The Rape of Lucrece* (1593–4), and is still evident in his latest plays, informing the dream visions of *Pericles* and *Cymbeline* and the masque in *The Tempest*, written between 1607 and 1611. It inflects his literary style throughout his career. In his earliest writings the verse, based on the ten-syllabled, five-beat iambic pentameter, is highly patterned. Rhetorical devices deriving from classical literature, such as alliteration and antithesis, extended similes and elaborate wordplay, abound. Often, as in *Love's Labour's Lost* and *A Midsummer Night's Dream*, he uses rhyming patterns associated with lyric poetry, each line self-contained in sense, the prose as well as the verse employing elaborate figures of speech. Writing at a time of linguistic ferment, Shakespeare frequently imports Latinisms into English, coining words such as abstemious, addiction, incarnadine and adjunct. He was also heavily influenced by the eloquent translations of the Bible in both the Bishops' and the Geneva versions. As his experience grows, his verse and prose become more supple, the patterning less apparent, more ready to accommodate the rhythms of ordinary speech, more colloquial in diction, as in the speeches of the Nurse in *Romeo and Juliet*, the characterful prose of Falstaff and Hamlet's soliloquies. The effect is of increasing psychological realism, reaching its greatest heights in *Hamlet*, *Othello*, *King Lear*, *Macbeth* and *Antony and Cleopatra*. Gradually he discovered ways of adapting the regular beat of the pentameter to make it an infinitely flexible instrument for matching thought with feeling. Towards the end of his career, in plays such as *The Winter's Tale*, *Cymbeline* and *The Tempest*, he adopts a more highly mannered style, in keeping with the more overtly symbolical and emblematical mode in which he is writing.

So far as we know, Shakespeare lived in Stratford till after his marriage to Anne Hathaway, eight years his senior, in 1582. They had three children: a daughter, Susanna, born in 1583 within six months of their marriage, and twins, Hamnet and Judith, born in 1585. The next seven years of Shakespeare's life are virtually a blank. Theories that he may have been, for instance, a schoolmaster, or a lawyer, or a soldier, or a sailor, lack evidence to support them. The first reference to him in print, in Robert Greene's pamphlet *Greene's Groatsworth of Wit* of 1592, parodies a line from *Henry VI, Part III*, implying that Shakespeare was already an established playwright. It seems likely that at some unknown point after the birth of his twins he joined a theatre company and gained experience as both actor and writer in the provinces and London. The London theatres closed because of plague in 1593 and 1594; and during these years, perhaps recognizing the need for an alternative career, he wrote and published the narrative poems *Venus and Adonis* and *The Rape of Lucrece*. These are the only works we can be certain that Shakespeare himself was responsible for putting into print. Each bears the author's dedication to Henry Wriothesley, Earl of Southampton (1573–1624), the second in warmer terms than the first. Southampton, younger than Shakespeare by ten years, is the only person to whom he personally dedicated works. The Earl may have been a close friend, perhaps even the beautiful and adored young man whom Shakespeare celebrates in his *Sonnets*.

The resumption of playing after the plague years saw the founding of the Lord Chamberlain's Men, a company to which Shakespeare was to belong for the rest of his career, as actor, shareholder and playwright. No other dramatist of the period had so stable a relationship with a single company. Shakespeare knew the actors for whom he was writing and the conditions in which they performed. The permanent company was made up of around twelve to fourteen players, but one actor often played more than one role in a play and additional actors were hired as needed. Led by the tragedian Richard Burbage (1568–1619) and, initially, the comic actor Will Kemp (d. 1603), they rapidly achieved a high reputation, and when King James I succeeded Queen Elizabeth I in 1603 they were renamed as the King's Men. All the women's parts were played by boys; there is no evidence that any female role was ever played by a male actor over the age of about eighteen. Shakespeare had enough confidence in his boys to write for them long and demanding roles such as Rosalind (who, like other heroines of the romantic comedies, is disguised as a boy for much of the action) in *As You Like It*, Lady Macbeth and Cleopatra. But there are far more fathers than mothers, sons than daughters, in his plays, few if any of which require more than the company's normal complement of three or four boys.

The company played primarily in London's public playhouses – there were almost none that we know of in the rest of the country – initially in the Theatre, built in Shoreditch in 1576, and from 1599 in the Globe, on Bankside. These were wooden, more or less circular structures, open to the air, with a thrust stage surmounted by a canopy and jutting into the area where spectators who paid one penny stood, and surrounded by galleries where it was possible to be seated on payment of an additional penny. Though properties such as cauldrons, stocks, artificial trees or beds could indicate locality, there was no representational scenery. Sound effects such as flourishes of trumpets, music both martial and amorous, and accompaniments to songs were provided by the company's musicians. Actors entered through doors in the back wall of the stage. Above it was a balconied area that could represent the walls of a town (as in *King John*), or a castle (as in *Richard II*), and indeed a balcony (as in *Romeo and Juliet*). In 1609 the company also acquired the use of the Blackfriars, a smaller, indoor theatre to which admission was more expensive, and which permitted the use of more spectacular stage effects such as the descent of Jupiter on an eagle in *Cymbeline* and of goddesses in *The Tempest*. And they would frequently perform before the court in royal residences and, on their regular tours into the provinces, in non-theatrical spaces such as inns, guildhalls and the great halls of country houses.

Early in his career Shakespeare may have worked in collaboration, perhaps with Thomas Nashe (1567–*c*. 1601) in *Henry VI, Part I* and with George Peele (1556–96) in *Titus Andronicus*. And towards the end he collaborated with George Wilkins (*fl*. 1604–8) in *Pericles*, and with his younger colleagues Thomas Middleton (1580–1627), in *Timon of Athens*, and John Fletcher (1579–1625), in *Henry*

VIII, *The Two Noble Kinsmen* and the lost play *Cardenio*.
Shakespeare's output dwindled in his last years, and he
died in 1616 in Stratford, where he owned a fine house,
New Place, and much land. His only son had died at the
age of eleven, in 1596, and his last descendant died in
1670. New Place was destroyed in the eighteenth century
but the other Stratford houses associated with his life are
maintained and displayed to the public by the Shakespeare
Birthplace Trust.

One of the most remarkable features of Shakespeare's
plays is their intellectual and emotional scope. They span
a great range from the lightest of comedies, such as *The
Two Gentlemen of Verona* and *The Comedy of Errors*, to
the profoundest of tragedies, such as *King Lear* and
Macbeth. He maintained an output of around two plays
a year, ringing the changes between comic and serious.
All his comedies have serious elements: Shylock, in *The
Merchant of Venice*, almost reaches tragic dimensions, and
Measure for Measure is profoundly serious in its examin-
ation of moral problems. Equally, none of his tragedies
is without humour: Hamlet is as witty as any of his comic
heroes, *Macbeth* has its Porter, and *King Lear* its Fool.
His greatest comic character, Falstaff, inhabits the history
plays and *Henry V* ends with a marriage, while *Henry
VI*, *Part III*, *Richard II* and *Richard III* culminate in the
tragic deaths of their protagonists.

Although in performance Shakespeare's characters can
give the impression of a superabundant reality, he is not
a naturalistic dramatist. None of his plays is explicitly
set in his own time. The action of few of them (except
for the English histories) is set even partly in England
(exceptions are *The Merry Wives of Windsor* and the
Induction to *The Taming of the Shrew*). Italy is his
favoured location. Most of his principal story-lines derive

from printed writings; but the structuring and translation of these narratives into dramatic terms is Shakespeare's own, and he invents much additional material. Most of the plays contain elements of myth and legend, and many derive from ancient or more recent history or from romantic tales of ancient times and faraway places. All reflect his reading, often in close detail. Holinshed's *Chronicles* (1577, revised 1587), a great compendium of English, Scottish and Irish history, provided material for his English history plays. The *Lives of the Noble Grecians and Romans* by the Greek writer Plutarch, finely translated into English from the French by Sir Thomas North in 1579, provided much of the narrative material, and also a mass of verbal detail, for his plays about Roman history. Some plays are closely based on shorter individual works: *As You Like It*, for instance, on the novel *Rosalynde* (1590) by his near-contemporary Thomas Lodge (1558–1625), *The Winter's Tale* on *Pandosto* (1588) by his old rival Robert Greene (1558–92) and *Othello* on a story by the Italian Giraldi Cinthio (1504–73). And the language of his plays is permeated by the Bible, the Book of Common Prayer and the proverbial sayings of his day.

Shakespeare was popular with his contemporaries, but his commitment to the theatre and to the plays in performance is demonstrated by the fact that only about half of his plays appeared in print in his lifetime, in slim paperback volumes known as quartos, so called because they were made from printers' sheets folded twice to form four leaves (eight pages). None of them shows any sign that he was involved in their publication. For him, performance was the primary means of publication. The most frequently reprinted of his works were the non-dramatic poems – the erotic *Venus and Adonis* and the more moralistic *The Rape of Lucrece*. The *Sonnets*, which appeared in 1609, under his name but possibly without his consent, were less successful, perhaps because the vogue for sonnet sequences, which peaked in the 1590s, had passed by then. They were not reprinted until 1640, and then only in garbled form along with poems by other writers. Happily, in 1623, seven years after he died, his colleagues John Heminges (1556–1630) and Henry Condell (d. 1627) published his collected plays, including eighteen that had not previously appeared in print, in the first Folio, whose name derives from the fact that the printers' sheets were folded only once to produce two leaves (four pages). Some of the quarto editions are badly printed, and the fact that some plays exist in two, or even three, early versions creates problems for editors. These are discussed in the Account of the Text in each volume of this series.

Shakespeare's plays continued in the repertoire until the Puritans closed the theatres in 1642. When performances resumed after the Restoration of the monarchy in 1660 many of the plays were not to the taste of the times, especially because their mingling of genres and failure to meet the requirements of poetic justice offended against the dictates of neoclassicism. Some, such as *The Tempest* (changed by John Dryden and William Davenant in 1667 to suit contemporary taste), *King Lear* (to which Nahum Tate gave a happy ending in 1681) and *Richard III* (heavily adapted by Colley Cibber in 1700 as a vehicle for his own talents), were extensively rewritten; others fell into neglect. Slowly they regained their place in the repertoire, and they continued to be reprinted, but it was not until the great actor David Garrick (1717–79) organized a spectacular jubilee in Stratford in 1769 that Shakespeare began to be regarded as a transcendental genius. Garrick's idolatry prefigured the enthusiasm of critics such as Samuel Taylor Coleridge (1772–1834) and William Hazlitt (1778–1830). Gradually Shakespeare's reputation spread abroad, to Germany, America, France and to other European countries.

During the nineteenth century, though the plays were generally still performed in heavily adapted or abbreviated versions, a large body of scholarship and criticism began to amass. Partly as a result of a general swing in education away from the teaching of Greek and Roman texts and towards literature written in English, Shakespeare became the object of intensive study in schools and universities. In the theatre, important turning points were the work in England of two theatre directors, William Poel (1852–1934) and his disciple Harley Granville-Barker (1877–1946), who showed that the application of knowledge, some of it newly acquired, of early staging conditions to performance of the plays could render the original texts viable in terms of the modern theatre. During the twentieth century appreciation of Shakespeare's work, encouraged by the availability of audio, film and video versions of the plays, spread around the world to such an extent that he can now be claimed as a global author.

The influence of Shakespeare's works permeates the English language. Phrases from his plays and poems – 'a tower of strength', 'green-eyed jealousy', 'a foregone conclusion' – are on the lips of people who may never have read him. They have inspired composers of songs, orchestral music and operas; painters and sculptors; poets, novelists and film-makers. Allusions to him appear in pop songs, in advertisements and in television shows. Some of his characters – Romeo and Juliet, Falstaff, Shylock and Hamlet – have acquired mythic status. He is valued for his humanity, his psychological insight, his wit and humour, his lyricism, his mastery of language, his ability to excite, surprise, move and, in the widest sense of the word, entertain audiences. He is the greatest of poets, but he is essentially a dramatic poet. Though his plays have much to offer to readers, they exist fully only in performance. In these volumes we offer individual introductions, notes on language and on specific points of the text, suggestions for further reading and information about how each work has been edited. In addition we include accounts of the ways in which successive generations of interpreters and audiences have responded to challenges and rewards offered by the plays. The Penguin Shakespeare series aspires to remove obstacles to understanding and to make pleasurable the reading of the work of the man who has done more than most to make us understand what it is to be human.

Stanley Wells

The Chronology of
Shakespeare's Works

A few of Shakespeare's writings can be fairly precisely dated. An allusion to the Earl of Essex in the chorus to Act V of *Henry V*, for instance, could only have been written in 1599. But for many of the plays we have only vague information, such as the date of publication, which may have occurred long after composition, the date of a performance, which may not have been the first, or a list in Francis Meres's book *Palladis Tamia*, published in 1598, which tells us only that the plays listed there must have been written by that year. The chronology of the early plays is particularly difficult to establish. Not everyone would agree that the first part of *Henry VI* was written after the third, for instance, or *Romeo and Juliet* before *A Midsummer Night's Dream*. The following table is based on the 'Canon and Chronology' section in *William Shakespeare: A Textual Companion*, by Stanley Wells and Gary Taylor, with John Jowett and William Montgomery (1987), where more detailed information and discussion may be found.

The Two Gentlemen of Verona	1590–91
The Taming of the Shrew	1590–91
Henry VI, Part II	1591
Henry VI, Part III	1591

Introduction

A Midsummer Night's Dream has long been one of Shakespeare's most popular and most studied plays. It is not hard to see why: in the first place, the very title is enticing, conjuring up balmy summer nights, romance and adventures in the realm of the imagination. On all these counts the play does not disappoint. Its fairy theme and its accessible comedy mean that it is often used as a first introduction to Shakespeare for children, while scholars have found in it a multi-layered complexity which gives ample scope to the pleasures of interpretation. To actors and directors it has offered inspiration for widely varying and inventive styles of production, as a play which itself has much to say about the processes, and the magic, of performance.

The play was composed at something of a transitional moment in Shakespeare's career. Like many of his plays, it cannot be dated precisely, but various kinds of evidence make it likely that it was written in around 1595 (see below, 'The ghosts of tragedy'). This places it after the early comedies (*The Two Gentlemen of Verona*, *The Taming of the Shrew*, *The Comedy of Errors* and *Love's Labour's Lost*), but just before the middle period of his career when Shakespeare wrote many of his most admired comedies (*The Merchant of Venice*, *Much Ado*

About Nothing, *As You Like It*, *Twelfth Night*). For some, it is one of Shakespeare's happiest, lightest plays, although others have found dark notes and themes in it, as will be explored below. Many acclaim it as a masterpiece; at the very least, it can be regarded as a play in which Shakespeare was aspiring to raise his comedy to new levels of artistry, seamlessly interweaving diverse strands of plot and theme. The play brings us not only slapstick and buffoonery from Bottom and the 'mechanicals' (working men) but also the courtly romantic foibles of the confusingly interchangeable Lysander and Demetrius, Hermia and Helena; it brings us not only the childish mischief-making of Puck but also deep reflection on the imagination and its workings, expressed especially eloquently in Theseus' speech at the closing wedding-feast. It is at once an entrancingly lyrical play and a play which provokes belly-laughs. It brings together motifs from Elizabethan court entertainments and from rural folklore. Its emblematic scene is perhaps that of the delicate, ethereal Titania, the Fairy Queen, embracing the hairy, clodhopping, ass-headed Bottom: we might regard this as a symbol of the union of mind and matter, of high art and popular entertainment, of imagination and the forms which it needs to take in order to be expressed and communicated.

OPENINGS

From its very first moments *A Midsummer Night's Dream* invites us to see things in at least two different ways. Theseus is impatient for his wedding to Hippolyta, the Amazon Queen whom he has won in conquest:

Now, fair Hippolyta, our nuptial hour
Draws on apace. Four happy days bring in
Another moon – but O, methinks how slow
This old moon wanes! She lingers my desires,
Like to a stepdame or a dowager
Long withering out a young man's revenue.

Hippolyta does not seem to share his impatience:

Four days will quickly steep themselves in night;
Four nights will quickly dream away the time:
And then the moon – like to a silver bow
New-bent in heaven – shall behold the night
Of our solemnities.

Here the woman is shown as in tune with the rhythms
and cycles of the moon, whereas the man aggressively
opposes himself to them. While Theseus personifies the
moon as 'a stepdame or a dowager', scornfully associating her with female decrepitude and dwindling fertility,
Hippolyta, as an Amazon, leader of a tribe of self-
governing, male-excluding women, has a natural affinity
with the moon goddess Diana, the chaste huntress, and
she accentuates this by her likening of the moon to a
bow such as Diana customarily carried.

The moon will appear again and again throughout the
play. It is a focal symbol for many key themes: its realm
is the night, the time for dreams and love; it is associated with lunacy, or madness, a state which many of the
characters will feel themselves to have passed through;
and it is associated with change. Through its monthly
fluctuations from darkness to crescent to full and back
again, the moon presents a universally recognizable

model of transformation, and this is a play full of transformations: from Bottom's metamorphosis into an ass, to Titania's conversion from rebellious wife to doting lover to reconciled spouse, to the human lovers' disorientating switches back and forth of desire until they settle down into happy couples. Even the flower which brings about those switches has been metamorphosed from white to purple to become a love-charm (II.1.166–8); even the human boy whom Oberon and Titania fight over is called a 'changeling' (23, 120). All the forces which animate the play – love, dreams, magic – are forces of transformation. And the moon, as well as being linked with all these forces and exemplifying change, also has both a dark phase and a bright phase; in this too it is a fitting motif for the whole play.

The ambivalence in the opening lines runs deeper than just Theseus' impatience opposed to Hippolyta's lack of it. What word, after all, *should* we use to describe her feelings? Is she serenely patient, merely soothing a beloved fiancé into waiting contentedly for a day to which she too is happily looking forward? Or is she angry and resentful, perhaps even a prisoner-of-war in chains, as some modern productions have depicted her? Theseus himself reminds both her and us, a few lines later, that 'I wooed thee with my sword, | And won thy love doing thee injuries' (I.1.16–17).

Another question which arises from these lines is why Theseus has to wait four days for his wedding. Presumably the mighty Duke of Athens can choose to get married whenever he likes. Perhaps the delay exists simply because we happen to be eavesdropping on the couple at this particular stage in lengthy preparations for pomp, triumph and revelling (I.1.19). Or, another answer might lie in the persistent moon imagery. In a pre-electric age, Elizabethans were far more conscious of the movements of the moon and stars than we are, and did indeed plan weddings and other important events carefully according to astrological prognostications. Natural functions were especially thought to be affected by the phases of the moon: a waxing moon was good for tasks which involved generation and growth, like the sowing of seeds or the breeding of animals, while a waning moon was good for tasks where retardation of regrowth or effusion was desirable, like nail-trimming or bloodletting. The dark of the moon was deemed to be inauspicious for any new endeavours, but especially marriages. Moreover, it was believed to coincide with women's menstrual periods, an idea hinted at in Hippolyta's language of 'steep[ing]' (7), and in the empurpling of the milk-white flower to become the love-charm (II.1.166–8), and again later in the staining with blood of Thisbe's mantle (V.1.274–5). The two latter instances might look primarily like metaphors for defloration: the flower is 'now purple with love's wound', and Pyramus/Bottom laments in malapropism that 'lion vile hath here deflowered my dear' (V.1.284). But menstruation and defloration are clearly linked as times of bleeding which mark the onset of a girl's sexuality, her transition from girl to woman, a transition with which this play is much concerned. Moreover, 'flowers' was the usual sixteenth-century term for menstrual blood.

Sex during the dark of the moon, during the woman's menstrual period, was regarded with horror in Shakespeare's time as unclean and likely to result in a malformed baby, what was termed a monstrous birth. The belief was that the menstrual matter in the womb would be fertilized to produce a misshapen lump of flesh, or a half-witted weakling, a 'moon-calf'. Various ancient

authorities were cited in support of this view, including
the Bible: 'menstruous women shall beare monsters' (2
Esdras 5:8, Apocrypha, Geneva Bible, 1560). The baby
might be born with bestial limbs or features, figuring
divine justice upon the parents for their bestial lust in
failing to control their sexual urges until a more fitting
time. The anxiety to avoid conceiving such a monster
has special bearing for Theseus, the vanquisher of the
Minotaur, the bull-headed man conceived by Pasiphae
in her intemperate lust for a beast. The perverse liaison
will be comically recalled in Titania's insatiable desire
for a man with the head of an ass. The transmuted Bottom
is at once like a bestial sexual partner and like the
deformed product of such a union; he is consistently
referred to as a 'monster' (III.1.98, III.2.6, 377).

Confusingly, the interval between Theseus' and
Hippolyta's opening speeches and the multiple wedding
which closes the play does not seem to be four days after
all. Later in the same first scene Lysander and Hermia
resolve to elope to the wood 'tomorrow night' (I.1.164);
that night forms the middle acts of the play, and they
wake from it at the end of Act IV to proceed directly to
the nuptials. Depending on how we count, this amounts
to three days at most; we might even feel it to be less,
experiencing the play as a day then a night then another
day. Some scholars have sought explanations for this, but
it is probably most sensible simply to see it as one of
Shakespeare's flexible time-schemes (*Othello* has another
notorious one) which refuse to submit to arithmetic.

The principal importance of the reference to 'four
days' in the opening speeches lies in the questions it raises
regarding the two speakers' attitudes to the delay. As we
have seen, various kinds of buried fears, tensions and
even antagonisms may be detected in their words – or

maybe not. Different readers or directors may bring their own interpretations to bear. This is crucial, since the decision as to how to play or read this moment sets the tone for all that follows. Theseus next speaks to Hippolyta after hearing Egeus's case against his disobedient daughter Hermia, and sentencing the girl, if she persists in resisting her father's marriage plan, 'To death or to a vow of single life.' He turns and says, 'Come, my Hippolyta. What cheer, my love?' (I.1.121–2). This could be merely a polite enquiry; perhaps he simply turns back from his business to recollect his bride, who has been passively looking on from the sidelines, and to ask 'Now, how are you?' Alternatively, since 'cheer' could mean the face, or a facial expression of mood, the line might indicate that the Amazon Queen's countenance shows displeasure at Theseus' patriarchal endorsement of a repressive law. Do the couple leave the stage arm in arm, or in opposite directions, completely at odds with one another?

We can read the play as opening either in a mood of light-heartedness and impending celebration which is merely ruffled by fleeting quarrels and quibbles, or in a mood of conflict, tension and hostility. This openness to diverse and even contradictory readings will continue throughout the play.

THE GHOSTS OF TRAGEDY

Darker notes may also be heard as we meet two more groups of characters, the young lovers and the mechanicals. As Hermia and Lysander lament their fate they run through all the different varieties of doomed love, agreeing that 'The course of true love never did run smooth' (I.1.134). A delicate balance of darkness and light is sustained; although the stories they invoke are tragic, they do so in a tone which is naive, formulaic, even slightly histrionic:

LYSANDER

. . . either it was different in blood –

HERMIA

O cross! – too high to be enthralled to low.

LYSANDER

Or else misgraffèd in respect of years –

HERMIA

O spite! – too old to be engaged to young.

LYSANDER

Or else it stood upon the choice of friends –

HERMIA

O hell! – to choose love by another's eyes. (I.1.135–40)

The passing backwards and forwards of lines here, very like a duet or a game, is in keeping with the entire role of the young lovers in the play, who will swap partners like performers of an elaborate geometric dance. Indeed, many readers and viewers find the lovers hard to distinguish, especially Lysander and Demetrius. Although there are distinctions of height and personality between the two young women, Helena at first wishes to be identical to Hermia, and later uses a striking image of symmetry to describe their girlhood intimacy: 'So we grew together | Like to a double cherry' (I.1.186–91, III.2.208–12). The indistinguishability of the lovers is no failure of characterization, but is in fact their whole point. A number of individual scenes rely for their comedy upon mistaking and on wooing the wrong person, and this is much the same effect as Shakespeare achieves in other comedies through the use of twins, as in *The Comedy of Errors* and

Twelfth Night. Lysander at the outset declares that his qualifications as a future husband are virtually identical to Demetrius'; but the crucial difference between them is that he is 'beloved of beauteous Hermia' (I.1.99–104). Throughout the lovers' plot, equally eligible candidates, indeed often the same candidate at different times, will inspire opposite and intense emotions, demonstrating that love is blind, mad, unfathomable and arbitrary.

At the same time, the doomed lovers from tales and histories to whom Lysander and Hermia compare themselves sound remarkably like a certain pair of star-crossed lovers with whom Shakespeare was much concerned at around this time. Both *A Midsummer Night's Dream* and *Romeo and Juliet* were probably composed some time in the mid 1590s. The *Dream* was mentioned by Francis Meres in a book called *Palladis Tamia* in 1598, and it was printed in 1600. There may be topical allusion in Titania's speech about bad weather and failed harvests (II.1.81–117): several poor harvests in the mid 1590s caused food shortages, and there were also several attacks of plague, which may be alluded to in Titania's mention of 'Contagious fogs' and 'rheumatic diseases' (90, 105). As mentioned above, most scholars date the play somewhere around 1595. Meanwhile, *Romeo and Juliet* was first printed in 1597, and scholars continue to debate how far before this it was written. We cannot be certain, then, which play came first; indeed, they might have been composed simultaneously. They are closely related in their lyricism and their interest in dreams and fairies (see Mercutio's 'Queen Mab' speech, *Romeo and Juliet*, I.4.53–103), as well as their concern with young love.

Their affinity is confirmed by the choice of play of the mechanicals: *Pyramus and Thisbe*. This story, taken from Ovid's *Metamorphoses* (transformations), bears

close similarity to *Romeo and Juliet*, both in its plot of
two lovers divided by their families and in its ending,
where mistakes, misunderstandings and mistimings – the
sort of devices we might more readily associate with
comedy – result in the young protagonists' suicides. The
spattered blood of Ovid's lovers was supposed to have
turned the fruit of the mulberry tree from white to purple,
a metamorphosis which accords with the other transformations in *A Midsummer Night's Dream*.

The points of resemblance or reverberation between
the two plays make it tempting to find in *A Midsummer
Night's Dream* a comic revisiting of, and commentary
upon, *Romeo and Juliet*. Even if, as many scholars think,
Romeo and Juliet was the later play, it is fascinating to
observe how the themes and motifs of the tragedy, often
thought of as one of the most poignant and pathos-filled
of Shakespeare's plays, seem to have been gestating in
his imagination during the composition of a comedy.

The full title of the inset play, as read out by Peter
Quince, describes it as a 'most lamentable comedy'; later
it will be presented at court as 'very tragical mirth' (I.2.11,
V.1.57). This partly parodies early Elizabethan plays
which often carried such title pages; *Cambyses* (by
Thomas Preston, 1569), for instance, was announced as
'A Lamentable tragedy mixed full of pleasant mirth'. But
here the mixing of generic labels runs deeper than just
mockery of foolish old plays, and deeper too than just
indicating that the mechanicals will make a ridiculous
botch of their performance. The close intertwining of
Pyramus and Thisbe, *Romeo and Juliet* and *A Midsummer
Night's Dream* illustrates how tragedy and comedy are
not entirely separate, as we might imagine, but rather
mutually interdependent. We can recognize a tragedy by
the offering of potential happy endings which are

violently snatched away; we can recognize that *A Midsummer Night's Dream* is a comedy by its being haunted, all the way through, by the tragedy which it might have been. At the end we can rejoice that Lysander and Helena turned out not to be Pyramus and Thisbe after all; this is a potent ingredient in the laughter we share with them at the mechanicals' play.

DIFFERENT WORLDS

In Act I we have met three successive groups of human characters. At the opening of Act II we are supposedly only a league or a mile away, in the wood outside Athens (again Shakespeare's specifications are inconsistent – see I.1.165, I.2.94); yet we find ourselves in another world completely, the world of the fairies. Shakespeare eases our movement between the different groups by mainly, though not exclusively, assigning a particular style to each: blank verse for Theseus and his court, couplets for the young lovers, prose for the mechanicals and lyrical poetry including song and dance for the fairies.

What kinds of creatures are the fairies? In nineteenth- and early-twentieth-century productions they were frequently played by children, or by ballerinas with tutus and gauzy wings; more recently they have been presented as muscular male trapeze-artists or punks or drug addicts. Scholarship suggests that, because Elizabethan playing companies were relatively small, in Shakespeare's own time the fairies were probably played by the same actors as the mechanicals (excepting Bottom). Within the text they seem to be sometimes tiny and delicate – one of the first ones we meet is on an errand to hang a dewdrop on every cowslip (II.1.8–15) – but at other times they appear to be of a similar size to mortals, and able to engage in love affairs with them, as in the accusations of infidelity which Oberon and Titania fling at one another (II.1.64–80). When Titania describes her friendship with the mother of the Indian boy there is no sense that the two women were markedly different in height, and indeed the changeling boy himself is described as 'little' by Oberon (120). The way in which the fairies need to tele-scope in size between different scenes and contexts, and the way in which we hardly notice this when watching or reading the play, is symptomatic of how the play as a whole engages our imaginations and sets them working collaboratively with the text.

Puck is very much a creature of English rural super-stition, a prankster who teases village maidens, milk-churning housewives and ale-drinking old wives (II.1.32–57). He goes by the names not only of Puck but also 'Robin Goodfellow' and 'Hobgoblin' (34, 40). Shakespeare probably knew about him from his own Warwickshire childhood, but could also have read about him in recent works like Reginald Scot's *Discovery of Witchcraft* (1584), or Thomas Nashe's *Terrors of the Night* (1594), both of which scoffed sceptically at what Nashe termed 'the Robin Goodfellows, elves, fairies, [and] hobgoblins of our latter age'. Shakespeare's character, as suggested by his alternative names, conflates several different types of mischief-making spirit. A puck was a type of small devil and a source of fear: the poet Edmund Spenser, in his *Epithalamion* (1595), a poem composed to celebrate his own wedding, invoked a blessing upon his bridal bed to be free of 'the Pouke', 'other evill sprights', 'mischivous witches' and 'hob Goblins', who might 'Fray us with things that be not' (ll. 341–4). Robin Goodfellow was viewed with a little less unease: his mischievous side was felt in practical jokes, in leading night-travellers out of their way, and in creating chaos in households which did not appease him; but he also benignly helped tidy and diligent maids and housewives by sweeping the floor and performing other domestic tasks during the night.

Puck, then, is very much a domestic, rural, native spirit. Yet Oberon has come to the wood 'from the farthest step of India', and Titania too is accustomed to disporting herself 'in the spicèd Indian air', the exotic realm of new explorations, imperial conquest and commerce, where she and her votaress have watched and mocked 'th'embarkèd traders on the flood' (II.1.69, 124, 127). Puck is a figure from the English past, Titania and Oberon figures from the alien lands looked to by the imperial, global future. In a modern work their equivalents would be creatures from outer space.

The name Oberon for the King of Fairies originated in a chivalric romance, *Huon of Bordeaux* (anon.), translated into English in around 1534 (by Sir John Bourchier, Lord Berners). According to this work Oberon's dominions lay to the east of Jerusalem, an area known to medieval writers as India, and he was about the height of a five-year-old child. A play based on the romance was staged in 1593. Oberon also appeared in Robert Greene's play of around 1590, *James the Fourth*, in which he was as small as the king on a playing card. Titania's name, by contrast, means daughter of Titans, that is, the giants who rebelled against the gods. It derives from Ovid's *Metamorphoses* – as we have already seen, an extensive influence on *A Midsummer Night's Dream* – where it occurs three times: once as a pseudonym for Diana, the moon goddess, in the story of Actaeon, whom she turned into a stag as punishment for accidentally seeing her naked; and twice as a pseudonym for Circe, the enchantress who turned men into beasts. Both stories of men transformed to animals have obvious resonance for the story of Titania and Bottom, though with the significant difference that in Shakespeare's version the transformation is not an act of power by a man-destroying enchantress but a disempowering humiliation of an enchantress by a higher male authority.

Even Puck can be seen as not only a spirit of the English countryside but also a version of a classical figure, Cupid, the mischievous boy love god, the 'knavish lad' who 'make[s] poor females mad' (III.2.440–41). What we see then, in Shakespeare's depiction of the fairies, is an extraordinarily rich mixing of diverse sources and traditions, native and exotic, low and high, ancient and modern. This is typical of the whole play. It is one of the few Shakespeare plays for which there does not seem to have been a direct primary source (others are *Love's Labour's Lost* and *The Tempest*). It can be classified as Shakespeare's own invention, yet he created it not out of 'airy nothing' (V.1.16), but by mixing elements of all sorts of different materials. A survey of such source materials would have to include, besides those I have already mentioned, the story of Balaam's ass in the Bible (Numbers 22), Seneca's *Hippolytus*, Plutarch's *Life of Theseus*, Apuleius' *Golden Ass*, Geoffrey Chaucer's dream-vision poems (especially the *Legend of Good Women*) and his *Knight's Tale* and *Tale of Sir Thopas* (*Canterbury Tales*, 1478), John Lyly's *Endymion* (1591), Spenser's *Faerie Queene* (1590–96), entertainments for Elizabeth I on her progresses, folk-tales of erotic encounters with the Fairy Queen, folk-rituals of maying and midsummer, dream-lore both popular and academic . . . and more. Yet most of us are completely unaware of this depth of background material when watching or reading the play. It has all been deftly woven by Shakespeare into a new, vibrant fabric which is entire of itself, and which can appeal to many different kinds of audience on many different levels.

OBERON AND TITANIA

The title of the play invites us to regard its nocturnal action, that is, the events of the middle three acts, as a dream. The fairy world, then, is also the world of fantasy. Whether we regard Theseus and Hippolyta as being at daggers drawn, or merely (to use modern terms) as having some issues which need to be resolved before their wedding, it is no great leap to see Oberon and Titania as in some sense their dream-personae. The doubling of their roles, whereby the actor playing Theseus also plays Oberon, and Hippolyta also plays Titania, which has become popular in modern productions, encourages such a reading. The fairy monarchs' dramatic entrance, sweeping in from opposite sides of the stage with their trains to confront one another, certainly seems to embody a battle of the sexes. Their contest swiftly becomes verbal as they deliver one of the most lyrical scenes in this very lyrical play, with both Oberon and Titania giving wonderful long speeches which are like operatic arias, or like word-pictures which entrance and inspire our imaginations.

The first of these is Titania's speech beginning 'These are the forgeries of jealousy', which widens into a vivid panorama of the disorder in nature which their quarrel has unleashed (II.1.81–117). As Titania fills in the word-picture with illustrative detail, we are once more in a very English countryside: 'The fold stands empty in the drownèd field . . . | The nine men's morris is filled up with mud' (I.1.96–8). This speech amplifies our sense of what the fairies are: they are forces of nature, beings invisible to us, superhuman yet subject to all-too-human emotional states which are responsible for the baffling cosmic vicissitudes to which mortals are subject. This resembles the world view of Ovid's *Metamorphoses*, where the very human passions and feuds of the gods have hazardous consequences for mortals.

Towards the end of Titania's speech, the language of fertility and procreation comes to the fore; but it is all failed fertility and procreation gone monstrously wrong. The 'childing autumn' has been aborted; Titania and Oberon's quarrel has produced a 'progeny of evils . . . We are their parents and original' (II.1.112–17). Literally speaking, the Fairy King and Queen are, of course, childless. Infertility and monstrous births are apt metaphors for failed harvests, distortion of the seasons and disruption of nature; but equally, medical books of Shakespeare's time commonly used the seasons, seed sowing and harvest as images and analogies for fertility and its failures. One very popular health manual, *The Birth of Mankind*, accounted for human barrenness as an imbalance of humours in the womb, which was too cold, moist, hot or dry. It illustrated this 'by a familiar example of sowing of corn':

For if it be sown in over-cold places . . . where the sun doth not shine, in these places the seed or grain sown, will never come to proof, nor fructify . . . And further, as concerning over-much humidity, if ye sow your grain in a fen or marsh and watery ground, the seed will perish through the over-much abundance of water, which extinguisheth the liveliness and the natural power of the grain and seed. (1598 edition)

Shakespeare himself uses seasonal and agricultural metaphors for human procreation in numerous places, such as Sonnet 3: 'where is she so fair whose uneared womb | Disdains the tillage of thy husbandry?'

Titania's language, then, may be read as expressing not only disorder in nature, but also her own infertility as the result, or the cause, or perhaps both, of her quarrel with Oberon. Certainly she displays all the symptoms which Elizabethan texts attributed to the hysteric, or sufferer from womb-sickness: rage, volatility, marital insubordination and sexual appetite. It may be that she has stolen the Indian boy, and holds on to him so fiercely, because her marriage has failed to give her her own child. In many ways, too, her later ministrations to Bottom seem to be less those of a lover than those of a surrogate mother, as she indulges all his needs to be fed, scratched and tickled, and lulls him to sleep in her embrace.

THE INDIAN BOY

In the contention over the Indian boy, as in the opening scene between Theseus and Hippolyta, we are again shown a couple who see things from two quite different angles. Even the account of how he came to be in Titania's possession is disputed. According to Puck, Oberon's follower, he was 'stolen from an Indian king' (II.1.22), but according to Titania, she has adopted him in loyal and affectionate memory of 'a votaress of my order' (123), who died in childbirth. These stories are diametrically opposed. Puck's version describes female despoliation of the property of a patriarch; Titania's version places the emphasis rather on bonds of love and intimacy between women. Both stories, though, sound subversively Amazonian, especially when we hear of how Titania and her resplendently pregnant votaress mocked the passing ships of the male mercantile world, whose 'big-bellied' sails were mere travesties of pregnancy, filled only with wind (II.1.127–9). The Indian woman was the Fairy Queen's votaress, avowed to her cause, much as a nymph of Diana or an Amazon would be bound by a pledge of service to a female leader. In return, Titania makes a pledge to her dead follower: 'And for her sake do I rear up her boy; | And for her sake I will not part with him' (136–7). The repetitive form and direct, simple language of these two lines make them like an incantation or a solemn oath. In a play about shape-shifting and shifting affections, they stand out as a resounding declaration of constancy. Of course this too will ultimately shift and dissolve; but at this point it is hard to see how Oberon can break down such obdurate female defences.

The boy himself, though at the centre of this conflict, remains a somewhat mysterious figure. He plays no part in the action, and he has no lines. Even so, many productions over the centuries have recruited a small boy to play him; or, in more recent productions, a virile youth. We have seen that we might find maternal feeling in Titania's care of Bottom; conversely, though, some readers have seen in her and Oberon's interest in the 'lovely boy' (II.1.22) as much sexual as parental motivation. Various productions (such as one directed by John Hirsch in Ontario in 1968; one by Danny Scheie for the Shakespeare Santa Cruz company in 1991; and David Pountney's 1995 English National Opera production of *The Fairy Queen*, Henry Purcell's semi-opera based on the play) cast the boy as an alluring adolescent who was clearly the object of libidinous designs of both fairy monarchs.

Whether a small boy in gilded robes or a virile youth

in a skimpy loincloth, the Indian boy is almost always presented in some way which visually marks him as 'exotic', non-European, non-white. A modern reader or spectator might find here some disturbing assumptions about racial 'others' as objects available for erotic purposes, or at least as emotional playthings or pets. The boy is given no subjectivity, no point of view within the play; he is entirely passive, significant only as a piece of property which is stolen, haggled over and finally surrendered to patriarchal authority. The language used about him is that of barter and trade: 'The fairy land buys not the child of me' (II.1.122). Many travel writings published in this period of exploration and nascent imperialism promoted a view that far-flung territories, like both the East and West Indies, were abundant sources of merchandise such as spices and jewels, which were simply lying around there waiting to be plundered and exploited. At the same time, 'Indian ware' was a proverbial expression for anything rare and costly which provoked desires to purchase and possess (see Sonnet 92 of Sir Philip Sidney's *Astrophil and Stella*, 1591). The treatment of the Indian boy by Oberon and Titania seems to reduce him to just such a commodity; and when he is shown onstage as a pretty, exotic, silent boy, of whatever age, he is served up as a commodity or eye-pleasing object for us too. Since he is not actually needed at all in performance, if he does appear it is as a decorative accessory. This treatment of the boy as a desirable bauble or trinket is reinforced by the way in which Titania speaks of his mother. Her womb was '*rich* with my young squire', and as well as mocking trading ships she also imitated them to bring her fairy mistress gifts, returning 'As from a voyage, rich with merchandise' (II.1.127–34). The boy has been her ultimate payment of tribute to her

Queen, and she was herself the vessel bearing him.

Such language implies colonialist attitudes: that far-flung territories and their inhabitants offer themselves to enrich and pleasure the colonizer. We may find such attitudes intolerable today; yet at the same time it must be acknowledged that this language of trade contributes to a radiant and sumptuous description of a pregnant woman, and a lyrical celebration of the fertile female body. To describe the unborn child in the Indian votaress's womb as 'riches' is not just materialistic, but also celebrates and admires her burden, especially when spoken by the childless Titania. The votaress sails across the yellow sands 'with pretty and with swimming gait', like a laden ship, vividly evoking the graceful and stately yet encumbered and swaying movement of a heavily pregnant woman. The 'spicèd Indian air by night' which she inhabits associates her with warmth, luxuriance and sensuality. Whereas Puck's version of the provenance of the Indian boy stresses the disruption of patrilineage, Titania's foregrounds the mother's role in gestation and birth, and does so in terms which forcefully accentuate and acclaim female physicality. As such it contrasts vividly both with Titania's own childlessness, and with another word-picture which follows closely: Oberon's vision of the 'imperial votaress', usually taken to be Elizabeth I, the Virgin Queen.

ELIZABETH I

Curiously, Shakespeare's works hardly ever mention Elizabeth I (1533–1603), the illustrious monarch who reigned for most of his life and who inspires enduring fascination to the present day. She ascended the throne in 1558, six years before Shakespeare's birth, and died in 1603, more than halfway through Shakespeare's writing career. Shakespeare's reticence about her contrasts with the way that most poets of the day, especially those with ambition, competed to produce ever more extravagant paeans of praise to Cynthia or Gloriana, as they fancifully entitled Elizabeth. Moreover, Shakespeare's theatrical company was the Lord Chamberlain's Men, whose named patron was the chief court official in charge of entertainments, and who were more frequently invited to perform at court than any other company, enjoying a prominent role as providers of plays for the Queen.

One of the few occasions when Shakespeare does refer directly to his Queen occurs in *A Midsummer Night's Dream*, and the moment comes as Oberon describes to Puck the genesis of the love-charm he wants him to fetch. He begins by recalling the song of a mermaid on a dolphin's back (II.1.148–54), a scene which resembles water-pageants for Elizabeth on her progresses to Kenilworth in 1575 and to Elvetham in 1591. He goes on:

> That very time I saw – but thou couldst not –
> Flying between the cold moon and the earth
> Cupid all armed. A certain aim he took
> At a fair vestal thronèd by the west,
> And loosed his loveshaft smartly from his bow
> As it should pierce a hundred thousand hearts;
> But I might see young Cupid's fiery shaft
> Quenched in the chaste beams of the watery moon,
> And the imperial votaress passed on
> In maiden meditation, fancy-free.
> Yet marked I where the bolt of Cupid fell:
> It fell upon a little western flower,
> Before, milk-white; now purple with love's wound. (155–67)

This 'imperial votaress', ruling an emergent empire, evidently avowed to chastity, immune to Cupid's arrow, radiant and ethereal, is unmistakably the Virgin Queen. The identification is confirmed by the prevalence of moon imagery both in this speech and throughout the play: the moon goddess, Cynthia or Diana, was a favourite poetic persona for Elizabeth, and indeed one of Shakespeare's few other apparent references to her is, after her death, as the 'mortal moon' (Sonnet 107).

Why does she turn up in *A Midsummer Night's Dream*? Since the early nineteenth century some scholars have speculated that the play might have been written for performance at an aristocratic wedding at which Elizabeth was expected to be present. This idea is based not only on the 'imperial votaress' speech, but on the inescapably strong nuptial theme of the play, and especially the culmination of this in the fairies' parting blessing:

> Now until the break of day
> Through this house each fairy stray.
> To the best bride bed will we,
> Which by us shall blessèd be;
> And the issue there create
> Ever shall be fortunate . . .
> Every fairy take his gait,
> And each several chamber bless
> Through this palace with sweet peace;
> And the owner of it blessèd
> Ever shall in safety rest. (V.1.391–6, 406–10)

By this closing phase the play has repeatedly crossed the boundaries between its different worlds, those of the fairies, the courtly lovers and the working-class amateur actors. It has also often positioned these different groups as spectators and performers, not only when the courtiers laugh at *Pyramus and Thisbe* in Act V, but also in the middle acts when Oberon and Puck observe as well as direct the travails of the mortals lost in the wood – 'Shall we their fond pageant see?' (III.2.114). The audience have watched the actors performing the role of audience; so at this moment, the actual actors might well turn to face the actual audience and cross a further boundary, the notional one that divides the stage from the real world. Was the 'house' or 'palace' referred to in this speech not simply Theseus' palace in Athens, but also the real house of an Elizabethan nobleman? Was he the 'owner' to be blessed, after the blessing of his daughter's marriage?

No fewer than eleven different Elizabethan court weddings have been put forward as possible occasions for the first performance of *A Midsummer Night's Dream*. Of these, the most probable is that of Elizabeth Carey to Thomas Berkeley on 19 February 1596. Elizabeth Carey was a favoured goddaughter of the Queen, named in honour of her royal godmother; her grandfather, Henry Carey, Lord Hunsdon, was the Lord Chamberlain, the patron of Shakespeare's company and the official in charge of providing theatrical entertainments at court. The family were Elizabeth I's closest surviving relations: Henry Carey's mother was Mary Boleyn, Anne Boleyn's sister, making him Elizabeth's first cousin – or even quite probably, since Mary had been Henry VIII's mistress before Anne, her half-brother. The Careys therefore seem prime candidates for the commissioning of a wedding-play in which a compliment to Elizabeth I would have been highly appropriate. There is also evidence in the family papers, and in other works dedicated to her, that Elizabeth Carey was known to have a personal interest in dreams.

The case remains unproven, however, and has provoked heated and continuing debate among scholars. Elizabethan court weddings were generally celebrated with masques (shorter, more formal, allegorical entertainments) rather than plays; and the documentary records of the Carey–Berkeley wedding make no mention of a play or of the Queen's presence. In any case, however, even advocates of the wedding theory do not dispute that the play would have been intended to run at the public playhouse after any wedding performance, in order to reap the maximum profit. Both sides of the argument agree that the play is remarkable for its ability to appeal to diverse audiences, combining learned allusions to authors like Ovid and Plutarch and motifs drawn from courtly literature with rural folklore and universally accessible farce.

We must leave unanswered the question of whether Elizabeth was either present, or expected to be present, at a performance. However, we can look again at the 'imperial votaress' speech to analyse how it represents her within the context of the play. It is true, as discussed above, that it uses the customary terms of 1590s court poetry, associating Elizabeth with the moon, foregrounding her virginity and representing her as a vision or divinity. But this moon is 'cold' and 'watery', recalling Theseus' threat to Hermia, in the play's first scene, of perpetual incarceration in a nunnery, 'Chanting faint hymns to the cold fruitless moon' (I.1.73). The view of virginity put forward there was unequivocally negative:

> But earthlier happy is the rose distilled
> Than that which, withering on the virgin thorn,
> Grows, lives, and dies in single blessedness. (76–8)

Virginity was presented as equivalent to death (121). In the same vein, the imperial votaress 'quenches' Cupid's arrow, suggesting a deadening, stifling effect, and she drifts rapidly off the scene, ghostlike and sterile, impervious to feeling or to the mortal vicissitudes which constitute most of the action of the play. This is a play primarily concerned with the transition from virginity to marriage, in which multiple marriages are presented as a resoundingly happy ending, and in which the 'quick bright things' of love and youth hold the stage (149). As such, the Virgin Queen has little place in it; indeed, the fleeting nature of her appearance indicates that she is there simply to exemplify the values in which the play is not interested, to outline by contrast its interest in the comic, the erotic and all the messier aspects of human emotion.

In fact one reason for the popularity of moon imagery in poetry ostensibly praising Elizabeth was its ambiguity. On the one hand, it could represent radiance, celestial transcendence and the virginity and divinity of Diana; on the other, it could imply unreliability, irrationality, nocturnal occult forces and the mysterious bodily cycles of women. As such it was extremely useful to poets who wished to be seen publicly to participate in loyal reverence towards the Queen, while more covertly signalling to the knowing reader their criticism of aspects of her rule. The many examples of such ambivalent writing include Sir Walter Ralegh's poem *The Ocean to Cynthia* (*c.* 1592) and parts of Spenser's *Faerie Queene*. The 1590s, the fourth decade of Elizabeth's reign, produced at once some of the most extravagant eulogies of her, and some of the most disgruntled rumblings of dissent. Poor harvests caused food shortages and soaring inflation, while the aristocratic elite got richer from their hold on trade monopolies. Meanwhile, controversy surrounding the capacity of a woman to rule resurfaced. The young men and militant Protestants of Elizabeth's court wanted her to pursue a more aggressive foreign policy against Catholic Spain, and her reluctance to do so, though largely based on financial shrewdness, was often blamed on the fact that she was an ageing woman. As such she was perceived as increasingly vacillatory in politics and fickle in her bestowal of personal favour, as in her turbulent on-off relationships with favourites such as Ralegh and Robert Devereux, the Earl of Essex.

If we do read the 'imperial votaress' passage as encodedly critical of the Queen, this need not preclude an original intention for it to be performed in her presence. Such multi-levelled imagery is found in much of the 1590s literature of her court. It may be that the covert expression of limited dissent was something Elizabeth tolerated, recognizing this as a useful release of pressure, behind the veil of gracious compliment graciously received.

Despite being antithetical to the themes of the play, the imperial votaress is also, however, crucial to the plot, since it is her immunity to Cupid's arrow which causes it to fall instead on the flower which becomes the love-charm. She is thereby responsible for Titania's lust for Bottom; in a sense, Elizabeth's repressed sexuality is displaced on to Titania. This raises many questions about the relations between the Virgin Queen and the Fairy Queen. Other figures of the Fairy Queen had appeared in entertainments presented to Elizabeth on her summer progresses, such as at Elvetham in 1591 (where 'Auberon, the Fairy King' was also mentioned); while in Edmund Spenser's *Faerie Queene*, whose first three books were published in 1590, Gloriana/Elizabeth was herself the

Queen of Fairyland. Clearly it would be rash to regard Titania as some sort of direct fictional personification of Elizabeth; to represent the Queen as an unruly wife humiliated by an erotic encounter with an ass-headed workman would go way beyond covert dissent to incur the perils of Elizabethan treason law. Yet some sort of association seems to have been recognized: in 1607 Thomas Dekker's allegorical play celebrating Elizabeth's defeat of Catholic enemies, *The Whore of Babylon*, had as its heroine 'Titania, the Fairie Queen, under whom is figured our late Queen Elizabeth'.

The narrative movement of Shakespeare's play, from unnatural chaos brought on by the assertion of female power, to order restored by the conversion of all the women into compliant wives, suggests a great deal about what he thought of female rule. Elizabeth's virginity was profoundly anomalous both in that it went against Protestant doctrine, which celebrated marriage as a high calling for a woman, and in that it gave her absolute power, unregulated by the higher male authority of a husband. The subtext of *A Midsummer Night's Dream* seems to be that this is an inversion of the natural order. Those women who strive for Amazonian autonomy, like Hippolyta and Titania, are firmly brought back into line under male husband-rulers.

THE WOOD

As Oberon directs Puck how to use the love-charm he speaks entrancingly of the 'bank where the wild thyme blows' where Titania sleeps (II.1.249). This speech, and the fairies' lullaby to Titania which opens the next scene, do much to establish the wood in our imaginations

(II.1.249–56, II.2.1–30). It is a place of floral abundance, of oxlips, violets, woodbine, and more, and it is teeming with animal life, with hedgehogs, newts, beetles and worms. Everything is animated: the violet is nodding, the snake is shedding her skin, the spiders are weaving. We are invited to see every detail, like the spots of the snakes and the long legs of the spiders, and to feel the leathern wings of the bats and the thorns of the hedgehogs. All this profusion and particularity has inspired some directors to seek to recreate the wood in detailed material form; one notorious example was Herbert Beerbohm Tree's 1911 revival of his 1900 production, in which live rabbits scampered around the stage. Shakespeare's own stage, however, was sparsely equipped; the purpose of his poetry is to evoke the wood in our imaginations. I have already mentioned several times above the influence upon the play of Ovid's *Metamorphoses*; as well as being felt in details of the play (such as the borrowing from Ovid of the story of *Pyramus and Thisbe*, or the use of his name Titania), and in its transformations (such as those of Bottom and of the flower which becomes the love-charm), this is also present in its depiction of nature as profusely alive and inhabited, since Ovid too showed a world in constant animation, peopled by the nymphs and sylphs of trees and springs.

Many of the animals mentioned by Shakespeare represent lurking dangers, whether the creepy-crawly sinisterness of spiders and beetles or the more substantial dangers of larger beasts. As the mortals enter the wood Demetrius threatens Helena with destruction by wild beasts or his own bestial cruelty (II.1.228, 214–19). Oberon hopes the waking Titania will look 'on lion, bear, or wolf, or bull, | On meddling monkey or on busy ape' (180–81), the reference to a bull recalling Pasiphae's bestial infatuation which produced the Minotaur (see p. xxvi). Animals are associated in the play with the dark, tragic forces which lurk on the edges of comedy, and with disorderly forces of lust which need to be redirected into the order of marriage. Imaginary bears, personifying all the looming, nebulous shapes thrown up by the unconscious, are mentioned no fewer than five times (II.2.36, 100; III.1.103–5; IV.1.112; V.1.22). Such repeated motifs are crucial to the poetic unity of the play. Even at its close the hungry lion still roars somewhere just out of sight (361).

One animal which takes on special emphasis is the snake or serpent. The fairies' lullaby wards off 'You spotted snakes with double tongue' (II.2.9), their adjectives not just precisely delineating the snakes in our imaginations but also implying inconstancy and duplicity. These associations intensify as Hermia wakes from her brief sleep to find Lysander gone:

> Help me, Lysander, help me! Do thy best
> To pluck this crawling serpent from my breast!
> Ay me, for pity! – What a dream was here!
> Lysander, look how I do quake with fear!
> Methought a serpent ate my heart away,
> And you sat smiling at his cruel prey.
> Lysander – what, removed? (151–7)

Although *A Midsummer Night's Dream* is full of dreamlike experiences, and indeed presents itself in its title and its epilogue as a dream, this is the only literal dream in the whole play. Shakespeare vividly recreates the experience of waking: the transition from the emotional arousal of the dream to sharpening awareness of the waking world; and the cryptic nature of the dream, its use of a language of symbols, which at once imply profound meaning yet resist interpretation. The urge to interpret is encouraged by the context of the dream. Dramatic irony creates pathos as Hermia wakes: we know, as she slowly realizes, that the Lysander to whom this speech is addressed is not there to hear it, and has abandoned her for Helena. The snake, with its traditional associations with deceit, seems to figure his treachery, as if Hermia has dreamed prophetically of events not yet known to her.

The snake had ancient associations with sexuality, both through its part in the biblical story of the Fall, and through its phallic shape. The event immediately preceding Hermia's sleep was a debate as Lysander anticipated open-air sex:

> One turf shall serve as pillow for us both;
> One heart, one bed, two bosoms, and one troth. (II.2.47–8)

Hermia fended him off, sustaining

> Such separation as may well be said
> Becomes a virtuous bachelor and a maid. (64–5)

In the rest of this exchange they both punned on the word 'lie', connoting both sexual intimacy in the sense of 'to lie with' and the deceitfulness of a snake. It is not hard to see the devouring snake of the ensuing dream as the threat of Lysander's sexual desire, which jeopardizes Hermia's honour and her bodily integrity. We may also see it, though, as figuring her own troubling sexual desire. Although she deters Lysander on this occasion, she has willingly put herself at extreme sexual risk by eloping to the wood, and has done so because she wishes to assert her own erotic desire over the will of her father.

Hermia's dream forms part of a recurring sequence of serpent imagery and related ideas through the play, from Lysander's early description of Demetrius as a 'spotted and inconstant man', to Hermia's vituperation of Demetrius as a serpent when she believes he has murdered Lysander, to Lysander's spurning of the clinging Hermia as a 'Vile thing' and 'serpent' (I.1.110; III.2.71–3, 260–61). Associations of sexuality, duplicity, infidelity and murderous intent cluster around the figure of the serpent. It is among various means whereby the sense of tragic potential which we saw initiated in Act I continues. Death is never far away. Helena risks rape at Demetrius' hands; Hermia avoids admitting to herself that Lysander might have been untrue by accusing Demetrius of having killed his rival; Helena threatens suicide; Lysander and Demetrius set out to duel with murderous intent (II.1.214–19; III.2.45–57, 244, 336–8). Helena's first thought on stumbling over the prone Lysander is 'Dead – or asleep?', a moment that will be echoed, but with an opposite answer to the question, when Thisbe discovers Pyramus's body: 'Asleep, my love? | What, dead, my dove?' (II.2.107, V.1.316–17). There is a degree of sadism both in the supposed lovers' and friends' threats and recriminations to one another, and in Oberon's treatment of Titania.

Yet all of this is managed with a lightness of touch which prevents us from taking it too seriously. For much of the play, especially in what should be their most emotionally intense moments, the lovers speak in rhyming couplets, maintaining that sense of their turmoils as an artificial game, and giving apt metrical form to the symmetries and asymmetries which organize them. At the same time their behaviour in the wood becomes increasingly absurd. Demetrius complains exasperatedly, 'And here am I, and wood within this wood', punning on 'wood' as an archaic word for 'mad' (II.1.192). The wood is a place where anything can happen, where individuals are pulled out of their usual social identities and relationships are pulled out of their usual alignments. As such, it is a place at once of disorientation and liberation, of confusion and discovery, of danger and play. It belongs to the genre of pastoral, used in many other Shakespeare plays, where characters are removed to an unfamiliar and uncivilized setting to undergo testing, revelatory, regenerative experiences before returning, with new insight, to the court or city from which they came. Other examples would include the Forest of Arden in *As You Like It*, or Bohemia in *The Winter's Tale*. In the *Dream* the presiding spirit of the wood is undoubtedly Puck, for whom 'those things do best please me | That befall preposterously' (III.2.120–21).

The love-charm renders the lovers not merely victims of this preposterousness, but active exponents of it. They often invoke reason, but usually to justify their most irrational actions, as when Lysander accounts for the conversion of his passion from Hermia to Helena:

The will of man is by his reason swayed,
And reason says you are the worthier maid.
Things growing are not ripe until their season;
So I, being young, till now ripe not to reason. (II.2.121–4)

Again dramatic irony is in force, as his earnestness is undercut by our knowledge that he is under narcotic influence. The play also seems to be saying something more general about the baffling rapidity with which young lovers can transfer their affections, and the emotional intoxications to which they are prone. This is accentuated by frequent references to eyes. Eyes are at once shining, beautiful features which inspire love (I.1.183, 230, 242; II.2.127; III.2.138–9) and the organs whereby beauty is perceived (I.1.56, III.1.132). There was debate in Shakespeare's time as to whether sight was produced by beams from the eye striking the object, or by beams from the object imprinting an image on the eye. Eyes could be active or passive; but in this play vision is almost always distorted or impeded in some way. It is no coincidence that the eye is the place where Oberon's love-charm is applied. We are told that 'Love looks not with the eyes, but with the mind' (I.1.234), but the distinction collapses as both eyes and mind are shown to be unreliable and inexplicable where love is concerned. Emphasizing this, a key word of the play is 'dote', a verb connoting both feebleness of mind and infatuation, and applied here to both Titania and the mortal lovers (108–9, III.2.3, IV.1.44, 46).

TITANIA AND BOTTOM

As the lovers act out their friendship-brawls and love-follies, the mechanicals arrive in the wood to rehearse, while Titania somehow sleeps onstage from II.2.30 to III.1.122. On the Elizabethan stage this was probably achieved using the discovery space, an alcove in the back wall of the stage. She wakes to set eyes, adoringly, on the ass-headed Bottom. What, exactly, happens between them? What does she have in mind when she orders her fairies to 'Lead him to my bower' (III.1.192)?

Jan Kott, in his book *Shakespeare Our Contemporary*, produced an influential reading of the play strongly inflected by the psychoanalytical ideas of Sigmund Freud. Kott followed the Freudian tendency to look for 'latent content' beneath the 'manifest content' of a story, and to find that buried latent content to be dark and sexual. He saw the *Dream* as 'the most erotic of Shakespeare's plays', heaving with images of perversion, decadence and grotesqueness, which centred around the bestial copulation between Titania and Bottom. For Kott the significance of Bottom's transformation was that 'since antiquity and up to the Renaissance the ass was credited with the strongest sexual potency and among all the quadrupeds is supposed to have the longest and hardest phallus'. Peter Brook's 1970 production for the Royal Shakespeare Company followed him in this sexual reading. The actors emphasized any potential bawdy pun; the depiction of Titania's encounter with Bottom, though far more festive and Dionysian than Kott's murky night-mare vision, was equally blatant in its carnality (see The Play in Performance). For Brook the true story of the play was 'a man taking his wife whom he loves totally and having her fucked by the crudest sex machine he can find' (*Plays and Players* 18, (1970)).

These readings might look like attention-seeking revi-sionism, engendered by the sexual revolution of the 1960s. However, even in Max Reinhardt's and William Dieterle's 1935 film of the play, Titania is dressed as a bride and she and Bottom process through floral arches to her bower to the accompaniment of the Wedding March from Felix Mendelssohn's incidental music for the *Dream* (1843): although couched decorously, what seems to be envisaged here is some kind of conjugal union. If we go back much further, too, to the *Golden Ass* of

Apuleius (born *c.* AD 114), one of the sources for the *Dream*, we find that the ass is a highly sexual creature. In this ancient Greek romance, translated into English by William Adlington in 1566, the hero transformed to an ass finds that he attracts various female admirers, including a lustful matron, who rhapsodizes over him much like Titania over Bottom: '"Thou art he whom I love, thou art he whom I only desire, without thee I cannot live" . . . Then she took me by the halter and cast me down upon the bed.' Despite his fear of hurting her with his great phallus, 'she eftsoons embraced my body round about, and had her pleasure with me, whereby I thought the mother of Minotaurus did not causeless quench her inordinate desire with a bull'.

If we go back to the text of the *Dream* itself, we can find plenty of sexual implications. Titania is woken by Bottom singing a 'cuckoo' song, implying that Oberon is about to be cuckolded; it also offers some of those potentially rude puns in its mention of cocks and quills (III.1.118–29). The names of some of the fairies who attend upon the lovers have sexual connotations. Bottom sends his compliments to Peaseblossom's father, Master Peascod (182): peascods, or pea-pods, were associated with love and sexuality in folk-magic, partly because of their shape (phallic and seed-filled), and partly because of the verbal inversion of the term codpiece (a piece of cloth in the crotch of a pair of men's breeches to cover or accentuate the genitals, so named because a cod was a bag of seeds). Mustardseed was valued as a folk remedy for its heat, and was prescribed to cure women of menstrual and uterine disorders. Midsummer's Eve was a favoured time for the most efficacious gathering and application of such herbal stimulants. Later, as Titania offers to wind Bottom in her arms, she rhapsodizes:

So doth the woodbine the sweet honeysuckle
Gently entwist; the female ivy so
Enrings the barky fingers of the elm. (IV.1.41–3)

A vine supported by an elm was a conventional emblem of a married couple; here, the variation to ivy suggests something amiss, but the imagery of physical entwinement and of phallic fingers being enringed strongly suggests copulation.

All of this seems to point in the direction of sexual action. We must not forget, though, that all Titania is urging Bottom to do as she winds him in her arms is to sleep. Moreover, when she first encountered him she seemed to have distinctly metaphysical forms of communion in mind: she likened his singing to an angel's voice, and declared that 'I will purge thy mortal grossness so | That thou shalt like an airy spirit go' (III.1.122, 151–2). Peter Quince, on first sight of Bottom with his ass's head, cries out, 'Bless thee, Bottom! Bless thee! Thou art translated!' (112–13) – a term which could mean not only reworded into another language, but conveyed to heaven without dying.

Bottom is the last of the mortals in the wood to wake, and when he does so it is to realize that he has 'had a most rare vision' (IV.1.203). As he goes on, he echoes and mangles a biblical text:

The eye hath not seen, and the ear hath not heard, neither have entered into the heart of man, the things which God hath prepared for them that love him. But God hath revealed them unto us by his spirit: for the spirit searcheth all things, yea, the deep things of God. (1 Corinthians 2:9–10, Bishops' Bible, 1572)

BOTTOM The eye of man hath not heard, the ear of man hath
    not seen, man's hand is not able to taste, his tongue to
    conceive, nor his heart to report what my dream was . . .
    It shall be called 'Bottom's Dream', because it hath no
    bottom. (IV.1.208–13)

His mismatching of organs and senses is at once funny
and in keeping with all the confusions of sight and sound
which have taken place in the wood (e.g. III.2.177–82),
and moreover profoundly expressive of the inexpress-
ibility of his dream. He says that 'man is but a patched
fool if he will offer to say what methought I had'
(IV.1.207–8), reminding us of the personification of
Folly in Erasmus's *Praise of Folly* (1509), who shows
that self-styled wisdom is often folly and apparent folly
is often wisdom, ideas directly influential upon
Shakespeare's later fool roles in *Twelfth Night*, *As You
Like It* and *King Lear*. Erasmus, drawing like Bottom on
1 Corinthians, even argued that Christ himself was a
kind of Holy Fool, and gave an eloquent description of
divine folly which sounds remarkably like what the
dreamers in Shakespeare's play have undergone:

'Eye has not seen nor ear heard, nor have there entered into
the heart of man the things which God has prepared for those
that love him.' . . . So those who are granted a foretaste of
this – and very few have the good fortune – experience something which is very like madness. They speak incoherently
and unnaturally, utter sound without sense, and their faces
suddenly change expression. One moment they are excited,
the next depressed, they weep and laugh and sigh by turns;
in fact they truly are quite beside themselves. Then when they
come to, they say they don't know where they have been, in

the body or outside it, awake or asleep. They cannot remember
what they have heard or seen or said or done, except in a mist,
like a dream. (Erasmus, *Praise of Folly* (trans. B. Radice,
1993))

Bottom seems to have had some kind of transcendental
revelation, and to have fleetingly touched the divine.

Many of the visual artists inspired by *A Midsummer
Night's Dream*, including Henry Fuseli in the 1790s,
Arthur Rackham in 1908 and Reinhardt in his 1935 film,
have dwelt upon the image of Bottom's huge, hairy,
clumsy ass-head cradled in the arms of the willowy,
ethereal, fragile Titania. The fascination of the image is
hard to articulate, but seems to lie somewhere in the
communion as well as contrast between the two figures,
a communion with all kinds of symbolic connotations
of the union of flesh and spirit, low and high, brutal and
tender. In the end we have to conclude that Shakespeare
leaves it entirely open whether or not they have sex.
Even if we think that they do, this does not mean that
we are limited to seeing their union as merely crude and
bestial. True, it would mean that Titania has sex with an
ass-headed mortal, which is undoubtedly a debasement,
but it also means that a humble mortal gets to make love
with the Fairy Queen – surely no ordinary sexual experience. Whatever passes between them, whatever form
of physical action we may imagine it to take, the chief
point about it is that the experience is revelatory and
transformatory – for both of them.

UNIONS, REUNIONS AND
AWAKENINGS

Titania no less than Bottom is changed when she awakes
from her enchantment. Her first words are 'My Oberon',
an endearing address that we have never heard her use
towards her spouse before (IV.1.75). 'New in amity',
they dance together; dancing and music are almost always
dramatic markers in Shakespeare's plays of ideal order
and magical resolution (84–6). Likewise Hippolyta, who
shortly reappears, seems reconciled to marriage to 'my
Theseus' (V.1.1); although she has been absent for the
middle acts, she seems to have been affected somehow
by the cure for unruliness worked upon Titania. Theseus,
too, who began the play bent on 'pomp' and 'triumph',
seems now to have come round to Hippolyta's view of
their wedding as a 'solemnity', to be observed with
contemplation and dignity as well as public ritual (I.1.11,
19; IV.1.87, 133, 184; V.1.359).

We are now moving from the relationship chaos of
the middle acts of the play to the harmony and conjugal
order of Act V. For the human lovers, this has meant
passing through some heated antagonisms, but always
organized under an overarching design of symmetries
and asymmetries. Lysander and Demetrius are entirely
consistent in being at each other's throats from Act I to
Act IV, but they are entirely inconsistent in their abrupt
switches of devotion from Hermia to Helena. Meanwhile
Hermia and Helena remain constant in the objects of
their love, but at the cost of sundering their girlhood
friendship. Their plot twists invite the drawing of a
geometrical diagram.

Helena conjures up an idyllic picture of her younger self and Hermia

> sitting on one cushion,
> Both warbling of one song, both in one key,
> As if our hands, our sides, voices, and minds
> Had been incorporate. (III.2.205–8)

Now we see them verbally sniping at each other, and, in some productions, resorting to considerable physical violence. Their 'schooldays' friendship, childhood innocence', even as they are imploringly extolled by Helena, are also nostalgically placed in the past (202). In this they resemble Titania's elegy for her Indian votaress. Bonds between women are evoked, and celebrated for their power, but only to be placed wistfully in the past and superseded by the higher adult calling of wifehood.

In the end the lovers resolve themselves into two symmetrical pairs, or a square: 'Two of both kinds makes up four' (III.2.438). Four was considered in ancient numerology to be the number of concord; the tetrad with its interlocking affinities and contraries was an emblem of the 'concord of this discord' at which the play has arrived (V.1.60). Puck sums up:

> Jack shall have Jill;
> Naught shall go ill.
> The man shall have his mare again, and all shall be well.
> (III.2.461–3)

This opposes another Shakespeare comedy composed very shortly before the *Dream*, *Love's Labour's Lost* (around 1594–5), which likewise seemed set to end with a multiple wedding, but was diverted from this track by news of a death and the consequent postponement of the weddings for a year. One of the suitors declared self-consciously, 'Our wooing doth not end like an old play; | Jack hath not Jill' (V.2.863–4). There, Shakespeare seemed to be testing and subverting comic conventions; but the *Dream*, on the contrary, revels in tying up ends exactly 'like an old play'.

This relies, however, on two devices. One is the fact that Demetrius is made into a happy bridegroom for Helena only by being left under the influence of the fairy enchantment. Some readers and spectators are troubled by this, but it is smoothed over in several ways. We can see the chopping-and-changing effects of the love-charm in the wood as, in any case, simply a heightened comic dramatization of the usual on-and-off, to-and-fro feelings of young lovers. We have also been told at the outset that Demetrius had been Helena's lover before transferring his attentions to Hermia at the urging of her father (I.1.106–14, 242–5), so the fairy-charm may be seen as merely returning him to his right mind and the true course of love from which he had been diverted.

Demetrius himself seems to be the most baffled, but simultaneously the most deeply affected, of all the waking lovers:

> Are you sure
> That we are awake? It seems to me
> That yet we sleep, we dream. (IV.1.191–3)

Several other characters in Shakespeare's earlier comedies had experienced comparable disorientating intermediate states. Antipholus of Syracuse in *The Comedy of Errors*, claimed as a husband by a strange woman who was, unbeknownst to him, wife to his lost twin brother, mused, 'Am I in earth, in heaven, or in hell? | Sleeping or waking? mad or well advised?' (II.2.222–3). Similarly in the frame-story which introduced *The Taming of the Shrew* the indigent tinker Christopher Sly, awoken from a drunken stupor to find himself dressed as a lord and apparently married to a lady, asked, 'Or do I dream? Or have I dreamed till now?' (Induction 2.68). More than two centuries later the poet John Keats, who found much inspiration in *A Midsummer Night's Dream*, would draw on Demetrius's plangent lines in his 'Ode to a Nightingale' (1819): 'Was it a vision, or a waking dream? | Fled is that music – do I wake or sleep?' (79–80). Keats relishes what Shakespeare again evokes so accurately and recognizably: the blurry, transitional, trance-like state of emerging from an intensely experienced dream without yet having fully entered the waking workaday world. Since he will never be released from the nocturnal love-charm, Demetrius, in a sense, will spend the rest of his life in this state. This is acceptable partly because it seems rather enviable, but also because as the play draws to a close Shakespeare is increasingly traversing or even dissolving the boundaries between the different worlds he has set up, as we shall see when we consider the epilogue.

As well as Demetrius' permanent enchantment, the other plot device needed to achieve a squaring-off is Theseus' change of heart. In Act I he had told Hermia sternly and utterly inflexibly that he could by no means extenuate the law of Athens (I.1.119–20). Now, though, he merely swats her protesting father aside:

Egeus, I will overbear your will;
For in the temple by and by with us
These couples shall eternally be knit. (IV.1.178–80)

His reversal can be accounted for partly by the dramatic needs and direction of the play, but also partly by character. The play shows the influence of Chaucer's *Knight's Tale* in its setting and in its motif of competing yet almost indistinguishable suitors, and in that work Theseus is given to similarly abrupt and capricious cancellations of previous edicts. The playwright also slips in before Theseus' reappearance the statement by Oberon – who might well overlap with Theseus in our minds – that at the ducal palace 'shall the pairs of faithful lovers be | Wedded with Theseus all in jollity' (90–91), rendering this a foregone conclusion even before the niceties of plot have been observed.

The play opened, then, with female desire tragically at odds with patriarchy. It ends with female desire and patriarchy mutually satisfied. There is the small problem of Egeus; Peter Brook's 1970 production sustained an unsettling note by showing Egeus as distinctly unreconciled to the end. But he has been overruled by a higher patriarchal power and is left isolated and disregarded amid the general overwhelming sense of alignment, harmony and resolution.

As Theseus and Hippolyta's hunting party stumbles upon the sleeping lovers, the Duke suggests that 'No doubt they rose up early to observe | The rite of May' (IV.1.131–2). This could simply be a joke about the couples persisting in love-games whose occasion is past; this is certainly the force of Theseus' invocation of another folk festival a few lines later: 'Saint Valentine is past! | Begin these woodbirds but to couple now?' (138–9). However, maying is alluded to elsewhere in the play too (e.g. I.1.166–7, III.2.296). May Morning marked the beginning of summer, and was traditionally celebrated by young people going into the countryside to gather branches of hawthorn blossom and bring them back into their towns and villages. It was a festival of nature brought into civilization, and of new growth and fertility; indeed, it was an occasion for courtship games, and was condemned by some preachers as a time of sexual licence. Yet our play seems from its title to be taking place on Midsummer's Eve, 23 June, St John's Eve – also a time of courtship customs, when various magical rituals were performed by young people to discover who they would marry. Once again making flexible use of the calendar, Shakespeare incorporates the associations of both occasions – and, even though it is said to be past, St Valentine's day too – creating a general sense of ephemeral festival time. Moreover, May Morning and Midsummer's Eve had in common a function as turning points: one the transition from spring to summer, the other the mid-point when early summer is over and we begin to look towards the fruition of summer's end. As such they are both highly appropriate as settings for the play's multiple transitions from maidenhood to wifehood.

PYRAMUS AND THISBE

Yet another affirmation of the happiness of the play's ending comes in the mechanicals' play, which, as we noted earlier, revisits the tragic potentialities of Act I of the *Dream*, but fulfils them in an absurd style which reduces them to laughter. The inset play serves another function, too: it invites us to think about plays themselves, and how they work.

We can learn a lot from the rehearsals and perform-ance of *Pyramus and Thisbe* about how Shakespeare's theatre operated. The constant heckling by the newly-

weds of the final performance of *Pyramus and Thisbe* in
Act V replicates the documented behaviour of young
gallants at the Elizabethan playhouse, who would sit in
prominent positions to be seen by the rest of the audience as much as to see the play and who regarded the
occasion as an opportunity to show off their wit. All the
parts on stage are of course taken by men, despite Flute's
reluctance to play Thisbe (I.2.43–4). In rehearsal Quince
becomes exasperated with Flute because 'You speak all
your part at once, cues and all' (III.1.92–3). Each actor
in an Elizabethan company would work not from a
complete text of the play, but from a script of his own
speeches only, punctuated by short tag-lines from the
preceding speeches of others to give him his cues. Flute
trundles on through this script as if it were continuous,
without waiting for Pyramus to speak his side of the
dialogue.

The 'tiring-house' which is mentioned was the
dressing room, which was at the back of the stage, and
whose front wall formed the stage backdrop. When the
actor playing Quince walks onstage and says, 'This green
plot shall be our stage, this hawthorn brake our tiring-
house' (III.1.3–4), several layers of irony are revealed.
An Elizabethan playhouse audience were being asked to
imagine that the actual stage and tiring-house were an
imaginary green plot and hawthorn thicket which the
actors would pretend were a stage and a tiring-house. In
such ways the mechanicals' play enabled Shakespeare to
expose and explore how the illusions of theatre work.
The mechanicals apply an earnest literalism: a wall must
be represented by a man in plaster and loam; the moon
must be represented by either the real moon shining in
through a window, or an actor playing the Man in the
Moon. In such instances they seem to have no concept

whatsoever of imagination. Paradoxically, though, in other instances they place too much faith in imagination, fearing that the ladies will truly believe Snug in costume to be a fearsome lion; to avert this, he must reassure them that he is not really a marauding beast, but only Snug the Joiner (III.1.27–65).

The function of the inset play is partly to enhance the framing play by contrast. The mechanicals personify an amateur and outdated approach to drama to which, it is implied, Shakespeare's company are vastly superior, not least in their skilled performance of the ineptness of the mechanicals. The mechanicals' methods intrude between us and the drama to prohibit the suspension of disbelief, whereas Shakespeare's seamless illusionism draws us in to participate in his art. We never really believe that Bottom is Pyramus – even in the most strained heights, or depths, of his performance he remains stubbornly Bottom – but we do accept in some sense that the actor playing Bottom is temporarily Bottom.

The actors of *A Midsummer Night's Dream* are all, in a sense, 'translated'; just as the metamorphosed Bottom is simultaneously an ass and a man, speaking language but also braying and craving oats, so all the cast are simultaneously themselves and the characters they play. This dualistic effect is intensified if we see a production with famous actors in the cast, and indeed in Shakespeare's time his company included individuals, like the clown Will Kemp who probably played Bottom, who had a following and were known as 'personalities' in their own right. Looked at from this angle, the mechanicals do more than simply fail at drama: in fact, they acknowledge and force us to acknowledge the willing duping we undergo to believe in fictional characters on stage, and the fact that acting is a form of falsehood. Bottom is clear that he will *play* Pyramus, not *be* Pyramus. What at first looked like lumpen-headed stupidity on their part can start to look more like acute attention to the processes of their art, against which we are the ones, like the heckling aristocrats, left looking rather foolish and shallow. Their dramatic self-consciousness and exposure of the processes of theatre are not all that far removed from what some modern playwrights would come to see as cutting-edge experimentalism.

A strong sense of the separation of drama from life determines the kind of language which Bottom and his friends use for their play. Here is no attempt at naturalism: the high tragedy to which they aspire requires a lofty style. Bottom's improvisation of 'raging rocks | And shivering shocks' (I.2.27–8) parodies the kind of 'stalking and roaring' performances popularized by the actor Edward Alleyn, renowned for his larger-than-life interpretations of roles like Marlowe's Tamburlaine, Faustus and Barabas, and star of the Lord Admiral's Company at the Rose playhouse from the late 1580s until his retirement in 1597. Contemporary comments indicate that the rival company, the Lord Chamberlain's Men, for which Shakespeare wrote, were coming to be known for a performance style which by contrast 'personated' character and 'painted' emotion in lifelike colours (see Andrew Gurr, *The Shakespearean Stage* (3rd edn, 1992). This was assisted by Shakespeare's prevalent use of iambic pentameter, usually unrhymed, a metre whose rhythms and line lengths have some resemblance to the inflections and phrasing of natural English speech. Here is Theseus speaking in iambic pentameter, but sounding quite conversational and naturalistic. He is commenting on Demetrius' inconstancy to Helena:

I must confess that I have heard so much,
And with Demetrius thought to have spoke thereof;
But, being overfull of self affairs,
My mind did lose it. But Demetrius, come;
And come, Egeus. You shall go with me. (I.1.111–15)

The young lovers, uncommonly for Shakespeare, sometimes speak in rhyme, as befits the formal patterning of
their amatory couplings and recouplings, and the sense
that in their youthfulness their ideas about love owe more
to poetry than experience. Hermia swears to Lysander:

By the simplicity of Venus' doves,
By that which knitteth souls and prospers loves,
And by that fire which burned the Carthage queen
When the false Trojan under sail was seen . . .
In that same place thou hast appointed me
Tomorrow truly will I meet with thee. (171–8)

Even in these rhymed lines the relatively light stresses
and the placings of pauses for breath of the iambic
pentameter approximate to the rhythm of colloquial
English speech.

Peter Quince prefers 'eight and six' (III.1.22), and
Pyramus and Thisbe as we finally see it is indeed
performed in lines of four, four and six syllables,
which like eight and six add up to units of fourteen.
'Fourteeners' were the preferred English metre of the
mid sixteenth century, but by the 1590s they were
becoming regarded as archaic and clumsy. Arthur
Golding had used the metre for his 1567 translation of
Ovid, which Shakespeare undoubtedly had to hand as
he wrote *A Midsummer Night's Dream*. A short burst of

Golding will illustrate how fourteeners can tend to bump along and to require some padding out of the line; and how this well-intentioned version of Ovid, successful in the terms of its own cultural moment, provided comic fuel for Shakespeare three decades later, and seems comic to us today. Here is Thisbe:

> Alas what chance my Pyramus hath parted thee and me?
> Make answer O my Pyramus: it is thy Thisb', even she
> Whom thou dost love most heartily that speaketh unto
>   thee . . .
> This said, she took the sword yet warm with slaughter
>   of her love
> And setting it beneath her breast, did to her heart it
>   shove. (IV.172–4, 196–7)

The rhythm is intrusive, and the lines feel somewhat flabby, filled out with superfluous banalities. It is a short step from this to Bottom and Flute's script. In fact, though, the comic note can be traced back even further than parody of Golding. Even in Ovid's original the tone often hovers uncertainly between high tragedy and absurd excess; we might suspect that Ovid is making fun of the lovers in the high-flown rhetoric he gives them and in the bathetic image he uses for Pyramus's spurting blood, which he describes in incongruous plumber's terms as like a jet of water from a burst pipe (*Metamorphoses*, IV.147–9).

IMAGINATION

In relation to *Pyramus and Thisbe*, *A Midsummer Night's Dream* is the real world; but only by means of the willing suspension of disbelief. Indeed, if we pursue a comparison between the two plays, they begin to look not so very unalike; merely in terms of plot, *Pyramus and Thisbe* might even be classed as more realistic than a story which asks us to believe in fairies and in a man's transformation to an ass.

The closing scenes of *A Midsummer Night's Dream* increasingly invoke the affinity between dream and theatre to inspire us to stretch our imaginations. A skilful and subtle dialogue is set up between scepticism and wonder. First Oberon announces that the lovers will 'think no more of this night's accidents | But as the fierce vexation of a dream' (IV.1.67–8). In this sentiment, despite being 'King of shadows', he sounds remarkably like the rationalist Theseus who will lightly dismiss the story of the night as 'fairy toys' (III.2.347, V.1.3). In fact the lovers, as much as Bottom, endearingly resist his injunction, and we feel inclined to do the same, complicit as we are in Oberon's higher knowledge of what has 'really' happened. In line with this, Titania is *not* permitted by Oberon to discard her nocturnal adventures as mere dream, but is confronted with the physical reality of her humiliation: 'There lies your love' (IV.1.77).

This all prepares for the dialogue between Theseus and Hippolyta which stands pivotally between the emergence from the wood and the mechanicals' performance. Typically for this play where so much is 'preposterous' – which literally means back-to-front or topsy-turvy – Theseus sets out to disparage imagination, but his speech turns in spite of itself into a celebration:

The poet's eye, in a fine frenzy rolling,
Doth glance from heaven to earth, from earth to heaven.

And as imagination bodies forth
The forms of things unknown, the poet's pen
Turns them to shapes, and gives to airy nothing
A local habitation and a name.

This account of 'shaping fantasies' uses metaphors of conception which are gracefully in keeping with the occasion of a wedding-night. It seems to attribute the poet with a godlike creative power, but deftly avoids authorial immodesty through being placed in the mouth of a sarcastic critic. Again there are layers of irony: Theseus is himself an 'antique fable' and an 'airy nothing', dependent for his existence and his voice upon the very poet's pen which he mocks (V.1.2–17).

At the opening of the play Theseus' impatience and attempted rationalism was balanced by Hippolyta's deeper affinity with and openness to the forces of night, magic and the imagination. Now she recognizes, musingly, that the 'story of the night' has 'transfigured' the minds of the lovers, and that it 'grows to something of great constancy; | But howsoever, strange and admirable' (V.1.23–7). The word 'admirable' literally means 'to be wondered at'. Wonder, not Theseus' 'cool reason' (V.1.6), is the keynote of the play. However uneasy he was about female rule, Shakespeare seems to have regarded the disempowered, like women, like the waking Bottom, as those more in tune with the forces of the imagination.

A radical stroke is the return of the fairies to close the play. We might have thought that when we and the Athenians returned from the wood, and from the middle acts of the play, we were returning to the real world, never to see the fairies again. However, in finally bringing the fairies into Theseus' palace, Shakespeare implies

that theirs is the higher reality, always there, circum-
scribing the world of imperceptive mortals. The action
ends with Oberon and Titania bestowing a blessing
through song and dance: 'Hand in hand with fairy
grace | Will we sing and bless this place' (V.1.389–90).
In performance we might experience this as a blessing
not only upon the fictitious couples and the house where
they sleep, but upon the playhouse and upon us, its
temporary inhabitants.

Fairies and actors have a special affinity. Oberon is
'King of shadows'; Theseus says of actors that 'The best
in this kind are but shadows' (III.2.347, V.1.208). Both
alike deal in illusions. It was a theme that Shakespeare
would return to at the end of his career, in *The Tempest*,
where Prospero's magic arts seem uncannily like the
powers of a playwright, and where the 'cloud-capped
towers' of both the stage and the world are said to be
equally evanescent. In that play we are told that 'We are
such stuff | As dreams are made on' (IV.1.148–57); in
the epilogue to *A Midsummer Night's Dream*, Puck comes
forward to invite us to view the whole play that we have
just witnessed as 'No more yielding but a dream'
(V.1.418).

As we have seen, both Oberon and Theseus decreed
that the lovers should dismiss their nocturnal adventures
as only dreams, but both these commands have met with
resistance from the characters of the play and from us,
so that Puck's apparent deprecation of the play as mere
dream instinctively provokes us to view it as much more.
This is a play fascinated by between-states: between sleep
and waking, between man and beast, between maiden-
hood and marriage, between tragedy and comedy. The
moonlight night is both light and dark (see V.1.264–7);
dreams are both truth and nonsense. The theatre, too, is

a place of pretence and of truth-telling, of play and of profundity, where 'everything seems double' (IV.1.189). Once again, as Puck turns to us, a boundary between worlds is traversed: he speaks across the divide between stage and spectators, and does so as a figure part-fairy still in costume and in role, part-actor about to remove his greasepaint and soliciting our applause. We have come out of the wood, out of the enclosing 'real world' of Athens, out of the further encircling world of the fairies, and we are about to emerge into the starkness and banality of our own real world, perhaps not without some questions as to just what 'reality' is. The epilogue invites us, like Bottom or Demetrius, to linger a moment longer in that reverie where we are not sure where the dream ends and waking begins.

Helen Hackett

The Play in Performance

Productions of *A Midsummer Night's Dream* have veered between the minimalist and the stupendously spectacular. In Shakespeare's own theatre scenery was sparse, so the audience's imaginations combined with the poetry would have done the work of creating Theseus' palace and the magical wood. As explained in the Introduction, the first performance of the *Dream* may possibly have been at an Elizabethan aristocrat's mansion, but we cannot be certain of this. We do know, though, from the 1600 title page of the play, that it was 'sundry times publicly acted' in the playhouse.

A visit to the modern Globe reconstruction on the South Bank of the Thames illustrates how the wooden pillars and beams of the Elizabethan playhouse might have lent themselves to imaginative use as forest trees. We know from surviving inventories that a neighbouring Elizabethan playhouse, the Rose, owned props such as 'moss banks' and 'a robe for to go invisible'. If Shakespeare's company had similar equipment, then such banks might have been used for Titania and the lovers to sleep upon, and such a robe might have been donned by Oberon at the line 'I am invisible' (II.i.186). The stage direction at III.i.96, 'Enter Puck, and Bottom with an ass's head', seems to refer to a specific company prop.

But Bottom's transformation and Oberon's invisibility, while they might be assisted by props, depend fundamentally upon our willing imaginative participation; and the stage would have been otherwise pretty bare. The cast would have been small, with the same actors probably playing the fairies and the mechanicals.

At the opposite extreme, Lucia Elizabeth Vestris's production of 1840, while restoring more of the text than had been performed for the preceding two hundred years, offered a populous cast and lavish scenic backdrops. These included a perspective view from Theseus's palace to the distant Acropolis, and a mist-filled forest featuring moonset and sunrise. There were fifty-two winged fairies dressed in white, gauze, spangled, ballet-style dresses, who glided in torch-bearing throngs along the galleries and staircases of Theseus' splendid palace for the closing blessing. These all swiftly became standard conventions for staging the play and endured well into the twentieth century.

Vestris's production, while in many ways distinctly Romantic, in fact ran against a certain tide of Romantic criticism. The essayist and critic William Hazlitt, on viewing a lavish operatic adaptation of the play, lamented, 'Oh, ye scene-shifters, ye scene painters, ye machinists and dress-makers, ye manufacturers of moon and stars that give no light . . . rejoice! This is your triumph; it is not ours' (*The Examiner*, 21 January 1816). Later, he concluded that 'Poetry and the stage do not agree well together'; that the play should only ever be read, allowing the imagination free rein – a rather problematic conclusion since Shakespeare obviously intended the play for the stage (*Characters of Shakespear's Plays*, 1817).

However, nineteenth-century directors ignored Hazlitt's admonitions and strove to outdo each other in spectacle. In various Victorian productions ships were used to convey Theseus into Athens at the opening of the play, or back from the wood to Athens at the end of Act IV, assisted by ingenious moving scenery. His palace became ever more gilded and ostentatious, and Charles Kean's 1856 production was thronged by no fewer than ninety fairies with coloured lanterns. Sir Herbert Beerbohm Tree in 1900 had mechanical birds singing in the forest trees, and his 1911 revival notoriously added real rabbits. New technologies were widely used to create illusion and add novelty. Gauzes and dioramas were used to create atmospheric effects, and electric lights were increasingly used to make the fairies glimmer like fireflies. Basil Dean's 1924 production at Drury Lane transported the requisite hordes of fairies up the monumental pillars of Theseus' palace by means of hydraulic lifts. All of this was often accompanied by Felix Mendelssohn's Romantic score, first incorporated into a production by Ludwig Tieck in 1843; the famous 'Wedding March' could be used for a splendid entrance procession of the three newly married couples in Act V.

Harley Granville-Barker in 1914 broke away from this illusionistic, sentimental tradition with a modernist production which used symbolist scenery, and depicted the fairies as gilded, oriental figures who moved like marionettes or living statues. Yet the Victorian tradition remained strong: as late as 1954 the Old Vic Theatre re-iterated the by now rather tired conventions of grandiose scenery and balletic dancing. The full-scale ballets based on the play by Balanchine (1962) and Ashton (1964) were equally neo-Romantic.

Peter Hall in 1959 used an Elizabethan-style set to attempt to refresh the play by returning it to its origins.

But the most radical break from Victorian conventions came with Peter Brook's 1970 Royal Shakespeare Company production. The set was a white box, above whose edges technical equipment was clearly visible, as were gantries from which cast members looked down to watch one another's performances. The few props were relatively abstract: suspended wire coils represented both the wood and the embroilments of passion. The cast deployed circus skills, like trapeze-swinging, stilt-walking and plate-spinning, to create an atmosphere of play and free physical movement. The text was uncut, whereas Victorian productions had often cut swathes of text to make way for spectacle. In total, including tours, the production had 535 performances in 36 cities, and, while controversial, was vastly influential.

In Brook's production Bottom's ass costume consisted merely of a black bulb nose, small black ears and black clogs. Some reviewers noted the resemblance to Mickey Mouse and felt disappointed by the departure from the more usual naturalistic fake ass's head, which in some productions has included elaborate mechanisms for working the mouth and making the ears and other features expressive. Such a prop, as I have said, is both naturalistic and fake: as Brook was clearly aware, the director's decision as to how physically ass-like to make Bottom goes to the centre of the play's own exploration of the relationship between illusion and reality. At the same time, exaggerated ass-like behaviour by Bottom, including braying, scratching and clumsiness, can add greatly to the visual humour of the play.

Brook's production innovated on other fronts too. Madame Vestris's 1840 production, in which she herself played Oberon, had established a convention, lasting until 1914, whereby Oberon was usually played by a woman. Such casting offered a glimpse of a handsome woman's legs, just as troupes of flimsily attired young women playing the fairies also offered titillating visual pleasures. Nevertheless, sexual content was carefully veiled or unacknowledged: Victorian productions cleaned up the text so that Hermia's 'virgin patent' became her 'maiden heart' (I.1.80), and Theseus instead of urging 'Lovers, to bed' merely exhorted 'Lovers, away' (V.1.354). The fairies often included numbers of children, casting an ambience of an innocent bedtime nursery-tale. Brook, however, brought sexuality to the fore (see Introduction, 'Titania and Bottom'). He doubled the roles of Theseus and Hippolyta with those of Oberon and Titania such as to invoke Sigmund Freud's interpretation of dreams as the place where repressed traumas and wish-fulfilment fantasies find expression. The doubling implies that Oberon and Titania are dream-personae for Theseus and Hippolyta, and that the middle acts represent the release and working out in the unconscious of the repressed tensions and desires of the waking world. Most strikingly, at the climax of Brook's production Bottom was carried to Titania's bower on the shoulders of her burly male fairies, one of whom thrust his fist upward between Bottom's legs to mimic a huge erection, while, icono-clastically, Mendelssohn's Wedding March played.

The doubling of the royal roles was not unprece-dented, but Brook's handling of it provoked discussion and established a modern convention. There were also lesser-known precedents for the introduction of upfront sexuality and 'sixties' styling. John Hancock's produc-tion in 1966 for the San Francisco Actor's Workshop was based on designs by the New York pop artist Jim Dine, which included a black, caged Hippolyta in leopardskin bikini and matching boots, a 6'4" man as Helena, and a costume based on the comic-book superhero Wonder Woman for Titania. This was originally intended to include rainbow-striped target circles on her breasts and two long thin light bulbs either side of her vagina. 'Let wires *show*!' noted Dine on his costume sketch, 'batteries *show*!' (Jim Dine, *Designs for 'A Midsummer Night's Dream'*, 1968).

Jan Kott's 1965 essay on the *Dream*, which viewed it as a dark, perverted, sexual fantasy, lay behind many modern sexual readings of the play. In fact disturbing tones had been found in the play since the 1790s, when the artist Henry Fuseli depicted a near-naked, voluptuous Titania draped around a huge, brawny Bottom, their attendants a mixed crowd of lascivious courtesans and little goblins. Max Reinhardt's stage productions of the 1930s and his film (with William Dieterle) of 1935 showed Bottom's experience as a nightmare from which he was mightily relieved to wake. Reinhardt made Oberon a distinctly forbidding king of shadows, and introduced a dance in which a sylph-like fairy is carried off by a man in black into the murky recesses of the forest. Robert Helpmann in 1937 and again in 1954 was a sinister androgynous Oberon (he would later play the Child-Catcher in the film of *Chitty-Chitty-Bang-Bang*). After Kott more violent extremes seemed possible, and Ariane Mnouchkine's 1968 production offered an Oberon who raped Hermia.

Other directors have been more mindful of the fact that the play is a comedy. One of the funniest ingredients in many productions is the verbal and then increasingly physical sparring among the four lovers, which rises to a climax in Act III, scene 2. The text tells us that Lysander tries to shake Hermia off as she clings to him, that Hermia flings herself at Helena to scratch her eyes out, that Demetrius and Lysander leave the stage 'cheek by jowl' to fight, and that Helena employs her long legs to run away (260–61, 297–8, 328, 338, 343). In performance this produces very effective visual comedy, while placing considerable physical demands on the actors, who will indeed collapse in an exhausted heap at the end of the scene. There is lots of humour in the escalating barrage of insults about the disparity in Hermia's and Helena's heights, which works especially well if the two actresses are indeed very different in stature (288–305, 325–30).

Other ingredients which customarily raise laughs from audiences include Puck's practical jokes, Titania's hyperbolic expressions of her infatuation with an ass and the scenes involving the mechanicals. Bottom and his friends have sometimes been played as mere buffoons, with lots of added slapstick; this was the case in Tree's production. Other productions, though, like Joseph Papp's which toured New York boroughs and schools in 1964, have presented them as simple but engaging exponents of some kind of authentic popular voice, who come off rather better than the condescending aristocrats who sneer with such feeble wit at their performance. Very frequently *Pyramus and Thisbe* is turned into a kind of perverse triumph, building into a potent mixture of the comic and the moving, as the mechanicals gradually win the audience over by their sheer wholeheartedness.

The inventiveness of recent directors has embraced the historical, the political, the psychoanalytical and the gothic. Robin Phillips at Ontario in 1976 and 1977 presented the whole play as dreamed by Elizabeth I, with Hippolyta and Titania suggesting two aspects of her personality, her resistance to patriarchal marriage and her fantasies of love-play. Meanwhile in Eastern Europe

in the 1970s and 80s the interest was in political topi-
cality, with various productions exploring the play as an
allegory of the struggle for freedom of imagination under
an oppressive regime. Back in England, Peter Hall's
productions of 1959 and 1962, and his 1969 film, accentuated the boisterous physical comedy between the quar-
relling lovers, who became increasingly mud-spattered;
Robert LePage went much further at the National
Theatre in 1992, with a set consisting of a pool and a
muddy bank, in and on which the characters descended
into violent wrestling and erotic couplings, such that the
front rows of the audience were issued with protective
waterproofs.

There were three notable productions in 2002. Richard
Jones at the RSC evoked gothic horror in a *black* box
set, swarmed over by fast-breeding flies and inhabited
by malignant drug-addled fairies. At Shakespeare's
Globe, by contrast, the play was a frolicsome slumber
party with all the cast in pyjamas and nighties, and the
fairies oversaw the mortal follies with tender and
beneficent curiosity. Lucy Bailey at Manchester's Royal
Exchange made inventive and good-humoured use of
audience participation and amusing props like mobile
phones, traffic cones, a white van and a tidily packed
Samsonite pull-along case for Hermia. The following
year, Peter Hall's son Edward directed an all-male
production at the Watermill Theatre in Newbury. This
was widely acclaimed as the most captivating interpretation for some time, with reviewers commenting less
on the cross-dressing than on the way the production
accentuated the magic and laughter of the play.

Reinhardt's film, mentioned above, is one of
numerous attempts to transfer the play to the screen. In
the silent era alone there were seven versions. Reinhardt

himself directed thirteen stage productions of the play between 1905 and 1934, including, after he fled Nazi Germany in the early thirties, one on epic scale in the vast open-air arena of the Hollywood Bowl before an audience of twelve thousand. His 1935 film is similarly dazzling in its visual display. It fascinatingly distils the sentimental tradition of child-fairies and ballet dancers, gauzy costumes (in this case ribboned Cellophane) and Mendelssohn's score, while introducing the darker undercurrents noted above. It also perpetuates the Victorian tradition of literalistic embodiment of the text's details, while showily deploying to this end the new technologies of film. The film's designer, Anton Grot, drew upon the fairy pictures of Gustave Doré (1832–83), giving them animated, three-dimensional form as hosts of fairies swarmed through the starry sky in ethereal spirals. We see Bottom's face metamorphose on screen from that of James Cagney to that of an ass; and when Puck says he will chase Bottom's friends as a hound, a hog and a fire (III.1.100–105) we are compelled to witness him taking all those forms.

Other cinematic versions have included Jiri Trnka's Czech puppet animation of 1959, Adrian Noble's 1996 film based on his Royal Shakespeare Company stage production, starring Alex Jennings and Lindsay Duncan, and Michael Hoffman's commercially aware version of 1999, with Rupert Everett and Michelle Pfeiffer. In 2001 Christine Edzard enterprisingly cast all the parts with eight-to-twelve-year-old children from south-east London; they are touching as well as sometimes slightly cringe-making for the viewer, much like the experience of watching a school play, and certainly refreshingly different from the usual thespian displays. The American high-school comedy *Get Over It* (Tommy O'Haver, 2001) has lots of fun with the *Dream*, in both its main plot and its own show-within-the-show.

Indeed, the *Dream* is remarkable not only for the wide polarities of interpretation it has provoked – from the minimalist to the sumptuously extravagant, from the flagrantly sexual to the chastely childlike, from the night-marishly dark to the radiantly joyful – but also for the numerous other works in other genres and media which it has inspired. As well as Mendelssohn's score and the ballets mentioned above, there have been Henry Purcell's semi-opera *The Fairy Queen* (1692), the 1939 American jazz-musical *Swingin' the Dream* with Louis Armstrong as Bottom, and Benjamin Britten's 1960 opera which stressed the homoerotic relationship between Oberon and Puck. Woody Allen's 1981 film *A Midsummer Night's Sex Comedy* paid homage to Shakespeare by way of Ingmar Bergman's *Smiles of a Summer Night*. And in 1998 *The Donkey Show* began an extended run off-Broadway, using seventies disco hits and a camp, raunchy style to tell the story of nightclub impresario Oberon, disco diva Titania and an illicit love-drug. Of course the play also remains a favourite for open-air performances, school plays and amateur productions, proving over and over again how magically it appeals to all audiences and breaks down barriers between high art and popular enter-tainment, just as it did in the 1590s.

Helen Hackett

Further Reading

A comprehensive guide to writings about *A Midsummer Night's Dream* up to 1986 is given by D. Allen Carroll and Gary Jay Williams's *'A Midsummer Night's Dream': An Annotated Bibliography*. Peter Holland's 1994 edition for the Oxford Shakespeare contains much valuable material, including a discussion of dream theory ancient and modern. Harold F. Brooks's Arden edition (1979) is especially comprehensive with regard to source materials, many of which are reprinted in the appendix, while R. A. Foakes's Cambridge edition (1984) is also good on sources and on stage history. Stanley Wells's article *'A Midsummer Night's Dream* Revisited' (*Critical Survey* 3 (1991), pp. 14–29) reviews discussion and interpretation of the play since his New Penguin Shakespeare edition of 1967.

Valuable older views of the play may be found in Harley Granville-Barker's *Preface* (1914; ed. Richard Eyre, 1993) and in *Shaw on Shakespeare* (ed. Edwin Wilson, 1961).

Kenneth Muir offers a resumé of sources in *The Sources of Shakespeare's Plays* (1977), many of which are reprinted in Geoffrey Bullough, *Narrative and Dramatic Sources of Shakespeare's Plays*, vol. I (1957). Jonathan Bate devotes a chapter to the *Dream* in *Shakespeare and Ovid* (1993).

The fullest exposition of the wedding theory about the first performance of the play is given by David Wiles in *Shakespeare's Almanac: 'A Midsummer Night's Dream', Marriage, and the Elizabethan Calendar* (1993), while its fullest refutation is given by Gary Jay Williams in *Our Moonlight Revels: 'A Midsummer Night's Dream' in the Theatre* (1997), which is also the most detailed stage history of the play. Other useful accounts of the performance history include Jay Halio's volume of 1995 for the Manchester University Press Shakespeare in Performance series, and Roger Warren's 1983 contribution to Macmillan's Text and Performance series.

Book-length studies of the play include David P. Young's *Something of Great Constancy: The Art of 'A Midsummer Night's Dream'* (1966), which illuminatingly explores the play in relation to Shakespeare's own ideas about his art; Stephen Fender's 1968 volume for Edward Arnold's Studies in English Literature series, which contains much insightful close reading; and James L. Calderwood's psychoanalytical study for the Harvester New Critical Introductions to Shakespeare series (1992). Helen Hackett's volume for the Writers and Their Work series (1997) discusses, among other things, the play's moon imagery, historical context, exploration of genre and depiction of nature. The *Dream* is at the centre of *The Purpose of Playing: Shakespeare and the Cultural Politics of the Elizabethan Theatre* by Louis Montrose (1996).

Montrose previously wrote a hugely influential essay on the play which exemplifies 'new historicist' criticism in reading the play alongside various 'non-literary' documents, such as a real Elizabethan dream about the Queen as recorded in a journal, and an ambassador's eye-witness account of Elizabeth I's physical appearance. It may be found in various places and versions, including '*A Midsummer Night's Dream* and the Shaping Fantasies of Elizabethan Culture: Gender, Power, Form', in Margaret W. Ferguson, Maureen Quilligan and Nancy J. Vickers (eds.), *Rewriting the Renaissance: The Discourses of Sexual Difference in Early Modern Europe* (1986), pp. 65–87. A slightly earlier version is reprinted in Richard Dutton's Macmillan New Casebook on the play (1986), along with a wide range of other essays usefully representing recent alternative critical viewpoints. Antony Price's 1983 Macmillan Casebook provides a range of extracts from earlier critical studies. Harold Bloom's collection for the Chelsea House Modern Critical Interpretations series (1987) includes an outstanding essay by Anne Barton, and Jan Kott's provocative essay on 'Titania and the Ass's Head'. The latter may also be found in Kott's *Shakespeare Our Contemporary* (English translation 1965).

Among books which included good chapters on the Dream are C. L. Barber, *Shakespeare's Festive Comedy: A Study of Dramatic Form and Its Relation to Social Custom* (1959); Marjorie Garber, *Dream in Shakespeare: From Metaphor to Metamorphosis* (1974); Philip C. McGuire, *Speechless Dialect: Shakespeare's Open Silences* (1985); William C. Carroll's *The Metamorphoses of Shakespearean Comedy* (1985); and Annabel Patterson, *Shakespeare and the Popular Voice* (1989). Stanley Wells wrote about 'Translations in *A Midsummer Night's Dream*' in *Translating Life: Studies in Transpositional Aesthetics* (ed. Shirley Crew and Alistair Stead, 1999). The chapter on *A Midsummer Night's Dream* by Helen Hackett in *The Blackwell Companion to Shakespeare's Works, Vol. III: The Comedies* (ed. Richard Dutton and Jean Howard, 2003) relates the play to Elizabethan theories of conception and fertility.

A MIDSUMMER
NIGHT'S DREAM

The Characters in the Play

THESEUS, Duke of Athens
HIPPOLYTA, Queen of the Amazons, betrothed to Theseus
EGEUS, Hermia's father
HERMIA, Egeus's daughter, in love with Lysander
LYSANDER, loved by Hermia
DEMETRIUS, suitor of Hermia
HELENA, in love with Demetrius
PHILOSTRATE, Theseus's Master of the Revels

OBERON, King of the Fairies
TITANIA, Queen of the Fairies
PUCK, or Robin Goodfellow
PEASEBLOSSOM
COBWEB
MOTH
MUSTARDSEED } Fairies

Peter QUINCE, a carpenter; Prologue in the interlude
Nick BOTTOM, a weaver; Pyramus in the interlude
Francis FLUTE, a bellows-mender; Thisbe in the interlude
Tom SNOUT, a tinker; Wall in the interlude
SNUG, a joiner; Lion in the interlude
Robin STARVELING, a tailor; Moonshine in the interlude

Other FAIRIES attending on Oberon and Titania
Lords and attendants to Theseus and Hippolyta

Enter Theseus, Hippolyta, Philostrate,
and attendants

THESEUS
    Now, fair Hippolyta, our nuptial hour
    Draws on apace. Four happy days bring in
    Another moon – but O, methinks how slow
    This old moon wanes! She lingers my desires,
    Like to a stepdame or a dowager
    Long withering out a young man's revenue.

HIPPOLYTA
    Four days will quickly steep themselves in night;
    Four nights will quickly dream away the time:
    And then the moon – like to a silver bow
    New-bent in heaven – shall behold the night   10
    Of our solemnities.

THESEUS   Go, Philostrate,
    Stir up the Athenian youth to merriments.
    Awake the pert and nimble spirit of mirth.
    Turn melancholy forth to funerals:
    The pale companion is not for our pomp. *Exit Philostrate*
    Hippolyta, I wooed thee with my sword,
    And won thy love doing thee injuries;
    But I will wed thee in another key:
    With pomp, with triumph, and with revelling.

Enter Egeus and his daughter Hermia, and Lysander,
and Demetrius

EGEUS

20   Happy be Theseus, our renownèd Duke.

THESEUS

Thanks, good Egeus. What's the news with thee?

EGEUS

Full of vexation come I, with complaint
Against my child, my daughter Hermia.
Stand forth, Demetrius! My noble lord,
This man hath my consent to marry her.
Stand forth, Lysander! – And, my gracious Duke,
This man hath bewitched the bosom of my child.
Thou, thou, Lysander, thou hast given her rhymes,
And interchanged love-tokens with my child.

30   Thou hast by moonlight at her window sung
With feigning voice verses of feigning love,
And stolen the impression of her fantasy.
With bracelets of thy hair, rings, gauds, conceits,
Knacks, trifles, nosegays, sweetmeats – messengers
Of strong prevailment in unhardened youth –
With cunning hast thou filched my daughter's heart,
Turned her obedience which is due to me
To stubborn harshness. And, my gracious Duke,
Be it so she will not here before your grace

40   Consent to marry with Demetrius,
I beg the ancient privilege of Athens:
As she is mine, I may dispose of her;
Which shall be either to this gentleman
Or to her death, according to our law
Immediately provided in that case.

THESEUS

What say you, Hermia? Be advised, fair maid:
To you your father should be as a god;

One that composed your beauties – yea, and one
To whom you are but as a form in wax
By him imprinted, and within his power   50
To leave the figure or disfigure it.
Demetrius is a worthy gentleman.

HERMIA

So is Lysander.

THESEUS   In himself he is;
But in this kind, wanting your father's voice,
The other must be held the worthier.

HERMIA

I would my father looked but with my eyes.

THESEUS

Rather your eyes must with his judgement look.

HERMIA

I do entreat your grace to pardon me.
I know not by what power I am made bold,
Nor how it may concern my modesty   60
In such a presence here to plead my thoughts;
But I beseech your grace that I may know
The worst that may befall me in this case
If I refuse to wed Demetrius.

THESEUS

Either to die the death, or to abjure
For ever the society of men.
Therefore, fair Hermia, question your desires,
Know of your youth, examine well your blood,
Whether, if you yield not to your father's choice,
You can endure the livery of a nun,   70
For aye to be in shady cloister mewed,
To live a barren sister all your life,
Chanting faint hymns to the cold fruitless moon.
Thrice blessèd they that master so their blood
To undergo such maiden pilgrimage;

But earthlier happy is the rose distilled
Than that which, withering on the virgin thorn,
Grows, lives, and dies in single blessedness.

HERMIA

So will I grow, so live, so die, my lord,
80   Ere I will yield my virgin patent up
Unto his lordship whose unwishèd yoke
My soul consents not to give sovereignty.

THESEUS

Take time to pause, and by the next new moon –
The sealing day betwixt my love and me
For everlasting bond of fellowship –
Upon that day either prepare to die
For disobedience to your father's will,
Or else to wed Demetrius, as he would,
Or on Diana's altar to protest
90   For aye austerity and single life.

DEMETRIUS

Relent, sweet Hermia; and, Lysander, yield
Thy crazèd title to my certain right.

LYSANDER

You have her father's love, Demetrius –
Let me have Hermia's. Do you marry him.

EGEUS

Scornful Lysander – true, he hath my love;
And what is mine my love shall render him;
And she is mine, and all my right of her
I do estate unto Demetrius.

LYSANDER

I am, my lord, as well derived as he,
100   As well possessed. My love is more than his,
My fortunes every way as fairly ranked –
If not with vantage – as Demetrius'.
And – which is more than all these boasts can be –
I am beloved of beauteous Hermia.

Why should not I then prosecute my right?
Demetrius – I'll avouch it to his head –
Made love to Nedar's daughter, Helena,
And won her soul; and she, sweet lady, dotes,
Devoutly dotes, dotes in idolatry
Upon this spotted and inconstant man.   110

THESEUS

I must confess that I have heard so much,
And with Demetrius thought to have spoke thereof;
But, being overfull of self affairs,
My mind did lose it. But Demetrius, come;
And come, Egeus. You shall go with me.
I have some private schooling for you both.
For you, fair Hermia, look you arm yourself
To fit your fancies to your father's will;
Or else the law of Athens yields you up –
Which by no means we may extenuate –   120
To death or to a vow of single life.
Come, my Hippolyta. What cheer, my love?
Demetrius and Egeus, go along;
I must employ you in some business
Against our nuptial, and confer with you
Of something nearly that concerns yourselves.

EGEUS

With duty and desire we follow you.

                    Exeunt all but Lysander and Hermia

LYSANDER

How now, my love? Why is your cheek so pale?
How chance the roses there do fade so fast?

HERMIA

Belike for want of rain, which I could well   130
Beteem them from the tempest of my eyes.

LYSANDER

Ay me! For aught that I could ever read,
Could ever hear by tale or history,

The course of true love never did run smooth;
But either it was different in blood –

HERMIA

O cross! – too high to be enthralled to low.

LYSANDER

Or else misgraffèd in respect of years –

HERMIA

O spite! – too old to be engaged to young.

LYSANDER

Or else it stood upon the choice of friends –

HERMIA

140   O hell! – to choose love by another's eyes.

LYSANDER

Or if there were a sympathy in choice,
War, death, or sickness did lay siege to it,
Making it momentany as a sound,
Swift as a shadow, short as any dream,
Brief as the lightning in the collied night,
That in a spleen unfolds both heaven and earth,
And – ere a man hath power to say 'Behold!' –
The jaws of darkness do devour it up.
So quick bright things come to confusion.

HERMIA

150   If then true lovers have been ever crossed
It stands as an edict in destiny.
Then let us teach our trial patience,
Because it is a customary cross,
As due to love as thoughts, and dreams, and sighs,
Wishes, and tears – poor fancy's followers.

LYSANDER

A good persuasion. Therefore hear me, Hermia:
I have a widow aunt, a dowager,
Of great revenue; and she hath no child.
From Athens is her house remote seven leagues;
160   And she respects me as her only son.

There, gentle Hermia, may I marry thee;
And to that place the sharp Athenian law
Cannot pursue us. If thou lovest me, then
Steal forth thy father's house tomorrow night,
And in the wood, a league without the town –
Where I did meet thee once with Helena
To do observance to a morn of May –
There will I stay for thee.

HERMIA   My good Lysander,
I swear to thee by Cupid's strongest bow,
By his best arrow with the golden head,   170
By the simplicity of Venus' doves,
By that which knitteth souls and prospers loves,
And by that fire which burned the Carthage queen
When the false Trojan under sail was seen,
By all the vows that ever men have broke –
In number more than ever women spoke, –
In that same place thou hast appointed me
Tomorrow truly will I meet with thee.

LYSANDER
Keep promise, love. Look – here comes Helena.
     Enter Helena

HERMIA
God speed, fair Helena! Whither away?   180

HELENA
Call you me fair? That 'fair' again unsay.
Demetrius loves your fair. O happy fair!
Your eyes are lodestars, and your tongue's sweet air
More tuneable than lark to shepherd's ear
When wheat is green, when hawthorn buds appear.
Sickness is catching. O, were favour so,
Yours would I catch, fair Hermia, ere I go.
My ear should catch your voice, my eye your eye,
My tongue should catch your tongue's sweet melody.

190 Were the world mine, Demetrius being bated,
The rest I'd give to be to you translated.
O, teach me how you look, and with what art
You sway the motion of Demetrius' heart.

HERMIA
I frown upon him, yet he loves me still.

HELENA
O that your frowns would teach my smiles such skill!

HERMIA
I give him curses, yet he gives me love.

HELENA
O that my prayers could such affection move!

HERMIA
The more I hate, the more he follows me.

HELENA
The more I love, the more he hateth me.

HERMIA
200 His folly, Helena, is no fault of mine.

HELENA
None but your beauty. Would that fault were mine!

HERMIA
Take comfort. He no more shall see my face.
Lysander and myself will fly this place.
Before the time I did Lysander see
Seemed Athens as a paradise to me.
O then, what graces in my love do dwell
That he hath turned a heaven unto a hell?

LYSANDER
Helen, to you our minds we will unfold.
Tomorrow night, when Phoebe doth behold
210 Her silver visage in the watery glass,
Decking with liquid pearl the bladed grass –
A time that lovers' flights doth still conceal –
Through Athens gates have we devised to steal.

HERMIA

And in the wood, where often you and I
Upon faint primrose beds were wont to lie,
Emptying our bosoms of their counsel sweet,
There my Lysander and myself shall meet,
And thence from Athens turn away our eyes
To seek new friends and stranger companies.
Farewell, sweet playfellow. Pray thou for us;   220
And good luck grant thee thy Demetrius.
Keep word, Lysander. We must starve our sight
From lovers' food till morrow deep midnight.

LYSANDER

I will, my Hermia.   *Exit Hermia*
                    Helena, adieu!
As you on him, Demetrius dote on you. *Exit Lysander*

HELENA

How happy some o'er other some can be!
Through Athens I am thought as fair as she.
But what of that? Demetrius thinks not so;
He will not know what all but he do know.
And as he errs, doting on Hermia's eyes,   230
So I, admiring of his qualities.
Things base and vile, holding no quantity,
Love can transpose to form and dignity.
Love looks not with the eyes, but with the mind,
And therefore is winged Cupid painted blind.
Nor hath love's mind of any judgement taste;
Wings and no eyes figure unheedy haste.
And therefore is love said to be a child
Because in choice he is so oft beguiled.
As waggish boys in game themselves forswear,   240
So the boy love is perjured everywhere;
For ere Demetrius looked on Hermia's eyne
He hailed down oaths that he was only mine,

And when this hail some heat from Hermia felt,
So he dissolved, and showers of oaths did melt.
I will go tell him of fair Hermia's flight.
Then to the wood will he tomorrow night
Pursue her; and for this intelligence
If I have thanks it is a dear expense.
250   But herein mean I to enrich my pain,
To have his sight thither, and back again.   *Exit*

I.2   *Enter Quince the carpenter, and Snug the joiner, and*
             Bottom the weaver, and Flute the bellows-mender,
             and Snout the tinker, and Starveling the tailor

QUINCE Is all our company here?

BOTTOM You were best to call them generally, man by
    man, according to the scrip.

QUINCE Here is the scroll of every man's name which is
    thought fit through all Athens to play in our interlude
    before the Duke and the Duchess on his wedding day at
    night.

BOTTOM First, good Peter Quince, say what the play treats
    on; then read the names of the actors; and so grow to a
10   point.

QUINCE Marry, our play is *The most lamentable comedy*
    and most cruel death of Pyramus and Thisbe.

BOTTOM A very good piece of work, I assure you, and a
    merry. Now, good Peter Quince, call forth your actors
    by the scroll. Masters, spread yourselves.

QUINCE Answer as I call you. Nick Bottom, the weaver?

BOTTOM Ready! – Name what part I am for, and pro-
    ceed.

QUINCE You, Nick Bottom, are set down for Pyramus.

20   BOTTOM What is Pyramus? – a lover or a tyrant?

QUINCE A lover that kills himself, most gallant, for love.

BOTTOM That will ask some tears in the true performing
of it. If I do it, let the audience look to their eyes! I will
move storms. I will condole, in some measure. To the
rest. – Yet my chief humour is for a tyrant. I could play
Ercles rarely, or a part to tear a cat in, to make all split:

> The raging rocks
> And shivering shocks
> Shall break the locks
>   Of prison gates,
> And Phibbus' car
> Shall shine from far
> And make and mar
>   The foolish Fates.

This was lofty! – Now name the rest of the players. –
This is Ercles' vein, a tyrant's vein. A lover is more
condoling.

QUINCE Francis Flute, the bellows-mender?

FLUTE Here, Peter Quince.

QUINCE Flute, you must take Thisbe on you.

FLUTE What is Thisbe? – a wandering knight?

QUINCE It is the lady that Pyramus must love.

FLUTE Nay, faith, let not me play a woman – I have a
beard coming.

QUINCE That's all one: you shall play it in a mask, and
you may speak as small as you will.

BOTTOM An I may hide my face, let me play Thisbe too.
I'll speak in a monstrous little voice: 'Thisne, Thisne!'
'Ah, Pyramus, my lover dear; thy Thisbe dear, and lady
dear.'

QUINCE No, no; you must play Pyramus; and Flute, you
Thisbe.

BOTTOM Well, proceed.

QUINCE Robin Starveling, the tailor?

STARVELING Here, Peter Quince.

QUINCE Robin Starveling, you must play Thisbe's
mother. Tom Snout, the tinker?

SNOUT Here, Peter Quince.

QUINCE You, Pyramus' father; myself, Thisbe's father;
60   Snug, the joiner, you the lion's part; and I hope here is
a play fitted.

SNUG Have you the lion's part written? Pray you, if it be,
give it me; for I am slow of study.

QUINCE You may do it extempore; for it is nothing but
roaring.

BOTTOM Let me play the lion too. I will roar that I will
do any man's heart good to hear me. I will roar that I
will make the Duke say 'Let him roar again; let him
roar again!'

70 QUINCE An you should do it too terribly you would fright
the Duchess and the ladies that they would shriek; and
that were enough to hang us all.

ALL That would hang us, every mother's son.

BOTTOM I grant you, friends, if you should fright the
ladies out of their wits they would have no more discretion but to hang us. But I will aggravate my voice so
that I will roar you as gently as any sucking dove. I will
roar you an 'twere any nightingale.

QUINCE You can play no part but Pyramus; for Pyramus
80   is a sweet-faced man; a proper man as one shall see in a
summer's day; a most lovely, gentlemanlike man. Therefore you must needs play Pyramus.

BOTTOM Well, I will undertake it. What beard were I
best to play it in?

QUINCE Why, what you will.

BOTTOM I will discharge it in either your straw-colour
beard, your orange-tawny beard, your purple-in-grain
beard, or your French-crown-colour beard, your perfect
yellow.

QUINCE Some of your French crowns have no hair at all; 90
and then you will play bare-faced! But, masters, here
are your parts, and I am to entreat you, request you, and
desire you to con them by tomorrow night, and meet me
in the palace wood a mile without the town by moonlight. There will we rehearse; for if we meet in the city
we shall be dogged with company, and our devices
known. In the meantime I will draw a bill of properties
such as our play wants. I pray you, fail me not.

BOTTOM We will meet, and there we may rehearse most
obscenely and courageously. Take pains, be perfect. 100
Adieu!

QUINCE At the Duke's oak we meet.

BOTTOM Enough; hold, or cut bowstrings.

Exeunt Bottom and his fellows

*

Enter a Fairy at one door, and Puck (Robin Good-   II.1
fellow) at another

PUCK

How now, spirit; whither wander you?

FAIRY

    Over hill, over dale,
        Thorough bush, thorough briar,
    Over park, over pale,
        Thorough flood, thorough fire –
    I do wander everywhere
    Swifter than the moon's sphere,
    And I serve the Fairy Queen,
    To dew her orbs upon the green.
    The cowslips tall her pensioners be;   10
    In their gold coats spots you see –

Those be rubies, fairy favours;
In those freckles live their savours.
I must go seek some dewdrops here,
And hang a pearl in every cowslip's ear.
Farewell, thou lob of spirits; I'll be gone.
Our Queen and all her elves come here anon.

PUCK

The King doth keep his revels here tonight.
Take heed the Queen come not within his sight,
For Oberon is passing fell and wrath
Because that she as her attendant hath
A lovely boy stolen from an Indian king.
She never had so sweet a changeling,
And jealous Oberon would have the child
Knight of his train, to trace the forests wild.
But she perforce withholds the lovèd boy,
Crowns him with flowers, and makes him all her joy.
And now they never meet – in grove or green,
By fountain clear or spangled starlight sheen –
But they do square, that all their elves for fear
Creep into acorn cups and hide them there.

FAIRY

Either I mistake your shape and making quite,
Or else you are that shrewd and knavish sprite
Called Robin Goodfellow. Are not you he
That frights the maidens of the villagery,
Skim milk, and sometimes labour in the quern,
And bootless make the breathless housewife churn,
And sometime make the drink to bear no barm,
Mislead night-wanderers, laughing at their harm?
Those that 'Hobgoblin' call you, and 'Sweet Puck',
You do their work, and they shall have good luck.
Are not you he?

PUCK   Thou speakest aright:

I am that merry wanderer of the night.
I jest to Oberon, and make him smile
When I a fat and bean-fed horse beguile,
Neighing in likeness of a filly foal;
And sometime lurk I in a gossip's bowl
In very likeness of a roasted crab;
And when she drinks, against her lips I bob,
And on her withered dewlap pour the ale.   50
The wisest aunt telling the saddest tale
Sometime for threefoot stool mistaketh me;
Then slip I from her bum. Down topples she,
And 'Tailor' cries, and falls into a cough;
And then the whole choir hold their hips and laugh,
And waxen in their mirth, and neeze, and swear
A merrier hour was never wasted there.
But room, Fairy: here comes Oberon.

FAIRY
And here my mistress. Would that he were gone!
Enter Oberon, the King of Fairies, at one door, with
his train; and Titania, the Queen, at another with hers

OBERON
Ill met by moonlight, proud Titania!   60

TITANIA
What, jealous Oberon? Fairy, skip hence.
I have forsworn his bed and company.

OBERON
Tarry, rash wanton! Am not I thy lord?

TITANIA
Then I must be thy lady. But I know
When thou hast stolen away from Fairyland
And in the shape of Corin sat all day
Playing on pipes of corn, and versing love
To amorous Phillida. Why art thou here
Come from the farthest step of India

70 But that, forsooth, the bouncing Amazon,
Your buskined mistress and your warrior love,
To Theseus must be wedded? – and you come
To give their bed joy and prosperity.

OBERON

How canst thou thus, for shame, Titania,
Glance at my credit with Hippolyta,
Knowing I know thy love to Theseus?
Didst thou not lead him through the glimmering night
From Perigenia, whom he ravishèd,
And make him with fair Aegles break his faith,
80 With Ariadne, and Antiopa?

TITANIA

These are the forgeries of jealousy;
And never since the middle summer's spring
Met we on hill, in dale, forest, or mead,
By pavèd fountain or by rushy brook,
Or in the beachèd margent of the sea
To dance our ringlets to the whistling wind,
But with thy brawls thou hast disturbed our sport.
Therefore the winds, piping to us in vain,
As in revenge have sucked up from the sea
90 Contagious fogs which, falling in the land,
Hath every pelting river made so proud
That they have overborne their continents.
The ox hath therefore stretched his yoke in vain,
The ploughman lost his sweat, and the green corn
Hath rotted ere his youth attained a beard.
The fold stands empty in the drownèd field,
And crows are fatted with the murrion flock.
The nine men's morris is filled up with mud,
And the quaint mazes in the wanton green
100 For lack of tread are undistinguishable.
The human mortals want their winter cheer.

No night is now with hymn or carol blessed.
Therefore the moon, the governess of floods,
Pale in her anger, washes all the air,
That rheumatic diseases do abound;
And thorough this distemperature we see
The seasons alter; hoary-headed frosts
Fall in the fresh lap of the crimson rose,
And on old Hiems' thin and icy crown
An odorous chaplet of sweet summer buds   110
Is as in mockery set. The spring, the summer,
The childing autumn, angry winter change
Their wonted liveries, and the mazèd world
By their increase now knows not which is which.
And this same progeny of evils
Comes from our debate, from our dissension.
We are their parents and original.

OBERON
Do you amend it, then! It lies in you.
Why should Titania cross her Oberon?
I do but beg a little changeling boy   120
To be my henchman.

TITANIA   Set your heart at rest.
The fairy land buys not the child of me.
His mother was a votaress of my order,
And in the spicèd Indian air by night
Full often hath she gossiped by my side,
And sat with me on Neptune's yellow sands
Marking th'embarkèd traders on the flood,
When we have laughed to see the sails conceive
And grow big-bellied with the wanton wind;
Which she with pretty and with swimming gait   130
Following – her womb then rich with my young squire –
Would imitate, and sail upon the land
To fetch me trifles, and return again

As from a voyage, rich with merchandise.
But she, being mortal, of that boy did die,
And for her sake do I rear up her boy;
And for her sake I will not part with him.

OBERON

How long within this wood intend you stay?

TITANIA

Perchance till after Theseus' wedding day.
140   If you will patiently dance in our round
And see our moonlight revels, go with us.
If not, shun me, and I will spare your haunts.

OBERON

Give me that boy and I will go with thee.

TITANIA

Not for thy fairy kingdom! Fairies, away.
We shall chide downright if I longer stay.

Exit Titania with her train

OBERON

Well, go thy way. Thou shalt not from this grove
Till I torment thee for this injury.
My gentle Puck, come hither. Thou rememberest
Since once I sat upon a promontory
150   And heard a mermaid on a dolphin's back
Uttering such dulcet and harmonious breath
That the rude sea grew civil at her song,
And certain stars shot madly from their spheres
To hear the sea-maid's music?

PUCK   I remember.

OBERON

That very time I saw – but thou couldst not –
Flying between the cold moon and the earth
Cupid all armed. A certain aim he took
At a fair vestal thronèd by the west,
And loosed his loveshaft smartly from his bow

As it should pierce a hundred thousand hearts;   160
But I might see young Cupid's fiery shaft
Quenched in the chaste beams of the watery moon,
And the imperial votaress passed on
In maiden meditation, fancy-free.
Yet marked I where the bolt of Cupid fell:
It fell upon a little western flower,
Before, milk-white; now purple with love's wound:
And maidens call it 'love in idleness'.
Fetch me that flower – the herb I showed thee once.
The juice of it on sleeping eyelids laid   170
Will make or man or woman madly dote
Upon the next live creature that it sees.
Fetch me this herb, and be thou here again
Ere the leviathan can swim a league.

PUCK
    I'll put a girdle round about the earth
    In forty minutes!   *Exit*
OBERON   Having once this juice
    I'll watch Titania when she is asleep,
    And drop the liquor of it in her eyes.
    The next thing then she, waking, looks upon –
    Be it on lion, bear, or wolf, or bull,   180
    On meddling monkey or on busy ape –
    She shall pursue it with the soul of love.
    And ere I take this charm from off her sight –
    As I can take it with another herb –
    I'll make her render up her page to me.
    But who comes here? I am invisible,
    And I will overhear their conference.
        Enter Demetrius, Helena following him
DEMETRIUS
    I love thee not, therefore pursue me not.
    Where is Lysander, and fair Hermia?

190   The one I'll slay; the other slayeth me.
    Thou toldest me they were stolen unto this wood,
    And here am I, and wood within this wood
    Because I cannot meet my Hermia.
    Hence, get thee gone, and follow me no more!

HELENA

    You draw me, you hard-hearted adamant!
    But yet you draw not iron: for my heart
    Is true as steel. Leave you your power to draw,
    And I shall have no power to follow you.

DEMETRIUS

    Do I entice you? Do I speak you fair?
200   Or rather do I not in plainest truth
    Tell you I do not nor I cannot love you?

HELENA

    And even for that do I love you the more.
    I am your spaniel; and, Demetrius,
    The more you beat me I will fawn on you.
    Use me but as your spaniel: spurn me, strike me,
    Neglect me, lose me; only give me leave,
    Unworthy as I am, to follow you.
    What worser place can I beg in your love –
    And yet a place of high respect with me –
210   Than to be usèd as you use your dog?

DEMETRIUS

    Tempt not too much the hatred of my spirit;
    For I am sick when I do look on thee.

HELENA

    And I am sick when I look not on you.

DEMETRIUS

    You do impeach your modesty too much,
    To leave the city and commit yourself
    Into the hands of one that loves you not;
    To trust the opportunity of night

And the ill counsel of a desert place
With the rich worth of your virginity.

HELENA

Your virtue is my privilege. For that   220
It is not night when I do see your face,
Therefore I think I am not in the night;
Nor doth this wood lack worlds of company,
For you in my respect are all the world.
Then how can it be said I am alone
When all the world is here to look on me?

DEMETRIUS

I'll run from thee and hide me in the brakes,
And leave thee to the mercy of wild beasts.

HELENA

The wildest hath not such a heart as you.
Run when you will. The story shall be changed: 230
Apollo flies, and Daphne holds the chase;
The dove pursues the griffin; the mild hind
Makes speed to catch the tiger – bootless speed,
When cowardice pursues, and valour flies.

DEMETRIUS

I will not stay thy questions. Let me go;
Or if thou follow me, do not believe
But I shall do thee mischief in the wood.

HELENA

Ay – in the temple, in the town, the field,
You do me mischief. Fie, Demetrius,
Your wrongs do set a scandal on my sex.   240
We cannot fight for love, as men may do;
We should be wooed, and were not made to woo.

                                        Exit Demetrius

I'll follow thee, and make a heaven of hell,
To die upon the hand I love so well.

                                        Exit Helena

OBERON

    Fare thee well, nymph. Ere he do leave this grove
    Thou shalt fly him, and he shall seek thy love.

    Enter Puck

    Hast thou the flower there? Welcome, wanderer.

PUCK

    Ay, there it is.

OBERON   I pray thee give it me.

    I know a bank where the wild thyme blows,
250   Where oxlips and the nodding violet grows,
    Quite overcanopied with luscious woodbine,
    With sweet muskroses and with eglantine.
    There sleeps Titania some time of the night,
    Lulled in these flowers with dances and delight.
    And there the snake throws her enamelled skin,
    Weed wide enough to wrap a fairy in.
    And with the juice of this I'll streak her eyes
    And make her full of hateful fantasies.
    Take thou some of it, and seek through this grove.
260   A sweet Athenian lady is in love
    With a disdainful youth – anoint his eyes;
    But do it when the next thing he espies
    May be the lady. Thou shalt know the man
    By the Athenian garments he hath on.
    Effect it with some care, that he may prove
    More fond on her than she upon her love.
    And look thou meet me ere the first cock crow.

PUCK

    Fear not, my lord; your servant shall do so.

                     Exeunt Oberon and Puck

Enter Titania, Queen of Fairies, with her train   II.2

TITANIA

    Come, now a roundel and a fairy song,
    Then for the third part of a minute hence:
    Some to kill cankers in the muskrose buds,
    Some war with reremice for their leathern wings
    To make my small elves coats, and some keep back
    The clamorous owl that nightly hoots and wonders
    At our quaint spirits. Sing me now asleep;
    Then to your offices, and let me rest.

    Fairies sing

FIRST FAIRY

        You spotted snakes with double tongue,
           Thorny hedgehogs, be not seen.   10
        Newts and blindworms, do no wrong,
           Come not near our Fairy Queen.

CHORUS

          Philomel with melody
          Sing in our sweet lullaby,
     Lulla, lulla, lullaby; lulla, lulla, lullaby.
            Never harm
            Nor spell nor charm
          Come our lovely lady nigh.
          So good night, with lullaby.

FIRST FAIRY

        Weaving spiders, come not here;   20
           Hence, you longlegged spinners, hence!
        Beetles black, approach not near,
           Worm nor snail, do no offence.

CHORUS

          Philomel with melody
          Sing in our sweet lullaby,
     Lulla, lulla, lullaby; lulla, lulla, lullaby.
            Never harm

Nor spell nor charm
Come our lovely lady nigh.
30   So good night, with lullaby.

Titania sleeps

SECOND FAIRY
Hence, away! Now all is well.
One aloof stand sentinel!

Exeunt Fairies

Enter Oberon
He squeezes the flower on Titania's eyes

OBERON
What thou seest when thou dost wake,
Do it for thy true love take;
Love and languish for his sake.
Be it ounce or cat or bear,
Pard, or boar with bristled hair
In thy eye that shall appear
When thou wakest, it is thy dear.
40   Wake when some vile thing is near!   *Exit*

Enter Lysander and Hermia

LYSANDER
Fair love, you faint with wandering in the wood;
And – to speak truth – I have forgot our way.
We'll rest us, Hermia, if you think it good,
And tarry for the comfort of the day.

HERMIA
Be it so, Lysander; find you out a bed,
For I upon this bank will rest my head.

LYSANDER
One turf shall serve as pillow for us both;
One heart, one bed, two bosoms, and one troth.

HERMIA
Nay, good Lysander, for my sake, my dear,
50   Lie further off yet; do not lie so near.

[handwritten annotations: "Hermia is tired", "Enters looking lost", "Admitting it", "For Decency's sake", "Wanting to be close to her", " BOSOMS – BODIES"]*

LYSANDER

O, take the sense, sweet, of my innocence!
Love takes the meaning in love's conference –
I mean that my heart unto yours is knit,
So that but one heart we can make of it.
Two bosoms interchainèd with an oath –
So then two bosoms and a single troth.
Then by your side no bed-room me deny,
For lying so, Hermia, I do not lie.

He didn't mean anything by it

He will respect HERMIA

HERMIA

Lysander riddles very prettily.
Now much beshrew my manners and my pride   60
If Hermia meant to say Lysander lied.
But, gentle friend, for love and courtesy
Lie further off, in human modesty:
Such separation as may well be said
Becomes a virtuous bachelor and a maid,
So far be distant, and good night, sweet friend;
Thy love ne'er alter till thy sweet life end.

LYSANDER

Amen, amen, to that fair prayer say I,
And then end life when I end loyalty.
Here is my bed: sleep give thee all his rest.   70

Doing what HERMIA wants

HERMIA

With half that wish the wisher's eyes be pressed.

Disappointed

They sleep
Enter Puck

PUCK

Through the forest have I gone,
But Athenian found I none
On whose eyes I might approve
This flower's force in stirring love.
Night and silence. – Who is here?
Weeds of Athens he doth wear.

This is he my master said
Despisèd the Athenian maid;
80   And here the maiden, sleeping sound
On the dank and dirty ground.
Pretty soul, she durst not lie
Near this lack-love, this kill-courtesy.
Churl, upon thy eyes I throw
All the power this charm doth owe.
He squeezes the flower on Lysander's eyes
When thou wakest let love forbid
Sleep his seat on thy eyelid.
So, awake when I am gone;
For I must now to Oberon.   *Exit*
Enter Demetrius and Helena, running

HELENA
90   Stay though thou kill me, sweet Demetrius!

DEMETRIUS
I charge thee hence; and do not haunt me thus.

HELENA
O, wilt thou darkling leave me? Do not so!

DEMETRIUS
Stay, on thy peril. I alone will go.   *Exit*

HELENA
O, I am out of breath in this fond chase.
The more my prayer, the lesser is my grace.
Happy is Hermia, wheresoe'er she lies,
For she hath blessèd and attractive eyes.
How came her eyes so bright? Not with salt tears –
If so, my eyes are oftener washed than hers.
100   No, no – I am as ugly as a bear;
For beasts that meet me run away for fear.
Therefore no marvel though Demetrius
Do as a monster fly my presence thus.
What wicked and dissembling glass of mine

Made me compare with Hermia's sphery eyne?
But who is here? – Lysander on the ground?
Dead – or asleep? I see no blood, no wound.
Lysander, if you live, good sir, awake!

LYSANDER (*wakes*)
And run through fire I will for thy sweet sake!
Transparent Helena, nature shows art   110
That through thy bosom makes me see thy heart.
Where is Demetrius? O, how fit a word
Is that vile name to perish on my sword!

HELENA
Do not say so, Lysander, say not so.
What though he love your Hermia, lord, what though?
Yet Hermia still loves you. Then be content.

LYSANDER
Content with Hermia? No, I do repent
The tedious minutes I with her have spent.
Not Hermia but Helena I love.
Who will not change a raven for a dove?   120
The will of man is by his reason swayed,
And reason says you are the worthier maid.
Things growing are not ripe until their season;
So I, being young, till now ripe not to reason.
And touching now the point of human skill,
Reason becomes the marshal to my will,
And leads me to your eyes, where I o'erlook
Love's stories written in love's richest book.

HELENA
Wherefore was I to this keen mockery born?
When at your hands did I deserve this scorn?   130
Is't not enough, is't not enough young man
That I did never – no, nor never can –
Deserve a sweet look from Demetrius' eye
But you must flout my insufficiency?

Good troth, you do me wrong – good sooth, you do –
In such disdainful manner me to woo.
But fare you well. Perforce I must confess
I thought you lord of more true gentleness.
O, that a lady of one man refused
140   Should of another therefore be abused!   *Exit*

LYSANDER
She sees not Hermia. Hermia, sleep thou there,
And never mayst thou come Lysander near.
For, as a surfeit of the sweetest things
The deepest loathing to the stomach brings,
Or as the heresies that men do leave
Are hated most of those they did deceive,
So thou, my surfeit and my heresy,
Of all be hated, but the most of me!
And, all my powers, address your love and might
150   To honour Helen and to be her knight.   *Exit*

HERMIA (*wakes*)
Help me, Lysander, help me! Do thy best
To pluck this crawling serpent from my breast!
Ay me, for pity! – What a dream was here!
Lysander, look how I do quake with fear!
Methought a serpent ate my heart away,
And you sat smiling at his cruel prey.
Lysander – what, removed? Lysander, lord!
What, out of hearing? Gone? No sound, no word?
Alack, where are you? Speak an if you hear.
160   Speak, of all loves! I swoon almost with fear.
No? Then I well perceive you are not nigh.
Either death or you I'll find immediately.   *Exit*

*

Enter the clowns: Bottom, Quince, Snout, Starveling, III.I
Flute, and Snug

BOTTOM Are we all met?

QUINCE Pat, pat; and here's a marvellous convenient place
for our rehearsal. This green plot shall be our stage, this
hawthorn brake our tiring-house, and we will do it in
action as we will do it before the Duke.

BOTTOM Peter Quince!

QUINCE What sayest thou, Bully Bottom?

BOTTOM There are things in this comedy of Pyramus and
Thisbe that will never please. First, Pyramus must draw
a sword to kill himself, which the ladies cannot abide.   10
How answer you that?

SNOUT By'r lakin, a parlous fear!

STARVELING I believe we must leave the killing out,
when all is done.

BOTTOM Not a whit. I have a device to make all well.
Write me a prologue, and let the prologue seem to say
we will do no harm with our swords, and that Pyramus
is not killed indeed; and for the more better assurance,
tell them that I, Pyramus, am not Pyramus, but Bottom
the weaver. This will put them out of fear.   20

QUINCE Well, we will have such a prologue; and it shall
be written in eight and six.

BOTTOM No, make it two more: let it be written in eight
and eight.

SNOUT Will not the ladies be afeard of the lion?

STARVELING I fear it, I promise you.

BOTTOM Masters, you ought to consider with yourself, to
bring in – God shield us – a lion among ladies is a most
dreadful thing; for there is not a more fearful wildfowl
than your lion living; and we ought to look to't.   30

SNOUT Therefore another prologue must tell he is not a
lion.

BOTTOM Nay, you must name his name, and half his face
must be seen through the lion's neck, and he himself
must speak through, saying thus, or to the same defect:
'Ladies', or 'Fair ladies – I would wish you', or 'I would
request you', or 'I would entreat you – not to fear, not to
tremble. My life for yours: if you think I come hither
as a lion, it were pity of my life. No. I am no such
thing. I am a man, as other men are' – and there indeed
let him name his name, and tell them plainly he is Snug
the joiner.

QUINCE Well, it shall be so. But there is two hard things:
that is, to bring the moonlight into a chamber – for, you
know, Pyramus and Thisbe meet by moonlight.

SNUG Doth the moon shine that night we play our play?

BOTTOM A calendar, a calendar! Look in the almanac –
find out moonshine, find out moonshine!

QUINCE Yes, it doth shine that night.

BOTTOM Why, then, may you leave a casement of the
Great Chamber window – where we play – open, and
the moon may shine in at the casement.

QUINCE Ay; or else one must come in with a bush of
thorns and a lantern, and say he comes to disfigure or to
present the person of Moonshine. Then there is another
thing. We must have a wall in the Great Chamber; for
Pyramus and Thisbe, says the story, did talk through the
chink of a wall.

SNOUT You can never bring in a wall. What say you,
Bottom?

BOTTOM Some man or other must present Wall; and let
him have some plaster, or some loam, or some roughcast
about him to signify Wall; and let him hold his fingers
thus, and through that cranny shall Pyramus and Thisbe
whisper.

QUINCE If that may be, then all is well. Come, sit down
   every mother's son, and rehearse your parts. Pyramus,
   you begin. When you have spoken your speech, enter
   into that brake; and so everyone according to his cue.

   Enter Puck

PUCK

   What hempen homespuns have we swaggering here   70
   So near the cradle of the Fairy Queen?
   What, a play toward? I'll be an auditor –
   An actor too, perhaps, if I see cause.

QUINCE Speak, Pyramus! Thisbe, stand forth!

BOTTOM *as Pyramus*

   Thisbe, the flowers of odious savours sweet –

QUINCE Odours – odours!

BOTTOM *as Pyramus*

                  . . . odours savours sweet.

   So hath thy breath, my dearest Thisbe dear.
   But hark, a voice. Stay thou but here awhile,
   And by and by I will to thee appear.   *Exit*   80

PUCK

   A stranger Pyramus than e'er played here.   *Exit*

FLUTE Must I speak now?

QUINCE Ay, marry must you; for you must understand he
   goes but to see a noise that he heard, and is to come
   again.

FLUTE *as Thisbe*

   Most radiant Pyramus, most lilywhite of hue,
      Of colour like the red rose on triumphant briar,
   Most brisky juvenal, and eke most lovely Jew,
      As true as truest horse that yet would never tire,
   I'll meet thee, Pyramus, at Ninny's tomb –   90

QUINCE 'Ninus' tomb', man! – Why, you must not speak
   that yet. That you answer to Pyramus. You speak all

your part at once, cues and all. Pyramus, enter – your
cue is past. It is 'never tire'.

FLUTE O!

(*as Thisbe*)

As true as truest horse, that yet would never tire.

Enter Puck, and Bottom with an ass's head

BOTTOM *as Pyramus*

If I were fair, fair Thisbe, I were only thine.

QUINCE O monstrous! O strange! We are haunted! Pray,
masters! Fly, masters! Help!

Exeunt Quince, Snug, Flute, Snout, and Starveling

PUCK

100   I'll follow you, I'll lead you about a round,

Thorough bog, thorough bush, thorough brake,
thorough briar,

Sometime a horse I'll be, sometime a hound,

A hog, a headless bear, sometime a fire,

And neigh, and bark, and grunt and roar and burn

Like horse, hound, hog, bear, fire at every turn. *Exit*

BOTTOM Why do they run away? This is a knavery of
them to make me afeard.

Enter Snout

SNOUT O Bottom, thou art changed. What do I see on
thee?

110   BOTTOM What do you see? You see an ass head of your
own, do you?

Exit Snout

Enter Quince

QUINCE Bless thee, Bottom! Bless thee! Thou art translated!   *Exit*

BOTTOM I see their knavery! This is to make an ass of me,
to fright me, if they could; but I will not stir from this
place, do what they can. I will walk up and down here,
and I will sing, that they shall hear I am not afraid.

   (*Sings*) The ousel cock so black of hue,
         With orange-tawny bill,
       The throstle with his note so true,   120
         The wren with little quill.

TITANIA (*wakes*)

   What angel wakes me from my flowery bed?

BOTTOM (*sings*)

       The finch, the sparrow, and the lark,
         The plainsong cuckoo grey,
      Whose note full many a man doth mark
         And dares not answer 'Nay'
  —for indeed, who would set his wit to so foolish a bird?
  Who would give a bird the lie, though he cry 'cuckoo'
  never so?

TITANIA

   I pray thee, gentle mortal, sing again!   130
   Mine ear is much enamoured of thy note.
   So is mine eye enthrallèd to thy shape,
   And thy fair virtue's force perforce doth move me
   On the first view to say, to swear, I love thee.

BOTTOM Methinks, mistress, you should have little reason
  for that. And yet, to say the truth, reason and love keep
  little company together nowadays – the more the pity
  that some honest neighbours will not make them friends.
  – Nay, I can gleek upon occasion.

TITANIA

   Thou art as wise as thou art beautiful.   140

BOTTOM Not so neither; but if I had wit enough to get out
  of this wood, I have enough to serve mine own turn.

TITANIA

   Out of this wood do not desire to go!
   Thou shalt remain here, whether thou wilt or no.
   I am a spirit of no common rate.
   The summer still doth tend upon my state,

And I do love thee. Therefore go with me.
I'll give thee fairies to attend on thee,
And they shall fetch thee jewels from the deep,
150   And sing while thou on pressèd flowers dost sleep;
And I will purge thy mortal grossness so
That thou shalt like an airy spirit go.
Peaseblossom, Cobweb, Moth, and Mustardseed!

Enter the four Fairies

PEASEBLOSSOM Ready!

COBWEB And I!

MOTH And I!

MUSTARDSEED And I!

ALL Where shall we go?

TITANIA
Be kind and courteous to this gentleman.
160   Hop in his walks and gambol in his eyes;
Feed him with apricocks and dewberries,
With purple grapes, green figs, and mulberries.
The honey bags steal from the humble bees,
And for night-tapers crop their waxen thighs
And light them at the fiery glow-worms' eyes
To have my love to bed and to arise;
And pluck the wings from painted butterflies
To fan the moonbeams from his sleeping eyes.
Nod to him, elves, and do him courtesies.

170 PEASEBLOSSOM Hail, mortal!

COBWEB Hail!

MOTH Hail!

MUSTARDSEED Hail!

BOTTOM I cry your worships mercy, heartily. I beseech
your worship's name.

COBWEB Cobweb.

BOTTOM I shall desire you of more acquaintance, good
Master Cobweb – if I cut my finger I shall make bold

with you! – Your name, honest gentleman?

PEASEBLOSSOM Peaseblossom.   180

BOTTOM I pray you commend me to Mistress Squash,
your mother, and to Master Peascod, your father. Good
Master Peaseblossom, I shall desire you of more acquaintance, too. – Your name, I beseech you, sir?

MUSTARDSEED Mustardseed.

BOTTOM Good Master Mustardseed, I know your
patience well. That same cowardly, giantlike Oxbeef
hath devoured many a gentleman of your house. I
promise you, your kindred hath made my eyes water
ere now. I desire your more acquaintance, good Master   190
Mustardseed.

TITANIA

Come, wait upon him. Lead him to my bower.
    The moon methinks looks with a watery eye;
And when she weeps, weeps every little flower,
    Lamenting some enforcèd chastity.
    Tie up my lover's tongue; bring him silently.

    Exit Titania with Bottom and the Fairies

    Enter Oberon, King of Fairies   III.2

OBERON

I wonder if Titania be awaked;
Then what it was that next came in her eye,
Which she must dote on, in extremity.
Here comes my messenger.
    Enter Puck
                            How now, mad spirit?
What night-rule now about this haunted grove?

PUCK

My mistress with a monster is in love.

Near to her close and consecrated bower,
While she was in her dull and sleeping hour,
A crew of patches, rude mechanicals
10 That work for bread upon Athenian stalls,
Were met together to rehearse a play
Intended for great Theseus' nuptial day.
The shallowest thickskin of that barren sort,
Who Pyramus presented, in their sport
Forsook his scene and entered in a brake,
When I did him at this advantage take.
An ass's nole I fixèd on his head.
Anon his Thisbe must be answerèd,
And forth my mimic comes. When they him spy —
20 As wild geese that the creeping fowler eye,
Or russet-pated choughs, many in sort,
Rising and cawing at the gun's report,
Sever themselves and madly sweep the sky —
So at his sight away his fellows fly,
And at our stamp here o'er and o'er one falls.
He 'Murder!' cries, and help from Athens calls.
Their sense thus weak, lost with their fears thus strong,
Made senseless things begin to do them wrong.
For briars and thorns at their apparel snatch,
30 Some sleeves, some hats. From yielders all things catch.
I led them on in this distracted fear,
And left sweet Pyramus translated there;
When in that moment — so it came to pass —
Titania waked, and straightway loved an ass.

OBERON

This falls out better than I could devise!
But hast thou yet latched the Athenian's eyes
With the love juice, as I did bid thee do?

PUCK

I took him sleeping — that is finished too;

And the Athenian woman by his side,
That when he waked of force she must be eyed.   40
    Enter Demetrius and Hermia

OBERON

Stand close. This is the same Athenian.

PUCK

This is the woman, but not this the man.

DEMETRIUS

O, why rebuke you him that loves you so?
Lay breath so bitter on your bitter foe.

HERMIA

Now I but chide; but I should use thee worse,
For thou, I fear, hast given me cause to curse.
If thou hast slain Lysander in his sleep,
Being o'er shoes in blood, plunge in the deep,
And kill me too.
The sun was not so true unto the day   50
As he to me. Would he have stolen away
From sleeping Hermia? I'll believe as soon
This whole earth may be bored, and that the moon
May through the centre creep, and so displease
Her brother's noontide with the Antipodes.
It cannot be but thou hast murdered him.
So should a murderer look; so dead, so grim.

DEMETRIUS

So should the murdered look, and so should I,
Pierced through the heart with your stern cruelty.
Yet you, the murderer, look as bright, as clear,   60
As yonder Venus in her glimmering sphere.

HERMIA

What's this to my Lysander? Where is he?
Ah, good Demetrius, wilt thou give him me?

DEMETRIUS

I had rather give his carcass to my hounds.

HERMIA

    Out, dog! Out, cur! Thou drivest me past the bounds
    Of maiden's patience. Hast thou slain him then?
    Henceforth be never numbered among men.
    O, once tell true – tell true, even for my sake.
    Durst thou have looked upon him being awake?
70   And hast thou killed him sleeping? O, brave touch!
    Could not a worm, an adder do so much?
    An adder did it; for with doubler tongue
    Than thine, thou serpent, never adder stung.

DEMETRIUS

    You spend your passion on a misprised mood.
    I am not guilty of Lysander's blood.
    Nor is he dead, for aught that I can tell.

HERMIA

    I pray thee, tell me then that he is well.

DEMETRIUS

    An if I could, what should I get therefore?

HERMIA

    A privilege never to see me more;
80   And from thy hated presence part I so.
    See me no more, whether he be dead or no.   *Exit*

DEMETRIUS

    There is no following her in this fierce vein.
    Here therefore for a while I will remain.
    So sorrow's heaviness doth heavier grow
    For debt that bankrupt sleep doth sorrow owe,
    Which now in some slight measure it will pay,
    If for his tender here I make some stay.
      He lies down and sleeps

OBERON

    What hast thou done? Thou hast mistaken quite,
    And laid the love juice on some true love's sight.
90   Of thy misprision must perforce ensue

Some true love turned, and not a false turned true.

PUCK

Then fate o'errules, that, one man holding truth,
A million fail, confounding oath on oath.

OBERON

About the wood go swifter than the wind,
And Helena of Athens look thou find.
All fancy-sick she is and pale of cheer
With sighs of love, that costs the fresh blood dear.
By some illusion see thou bring her here.
I'll charm his eyes against she do appear.

PUCK

I go, I go – look how I go –   100
Swifter than arrow from the Tartar's bow.   *Exit*

OBERON

Flower of this purple dye,
Hit with Cupid's archery,
Sink in apple of his eye.
He squeezes the flower on Demetrius's eyes
When his love he doth espy,
Let her shine as gloriously
As the Venus of the sky.
When thou wakest, if she be by,
Beg of her for remedy.
Enter Puck

PUCK

Captain of our fairy band,   110
Helena is here at hand,
And the youth mistook by me,
Pleading for a lover's fee.
Shall we their fond pageant see?
Lord, what fools these mortals be!

OBERON

Stand aside. The noise they make

Will cause Demetrius to awake.

PUCK

    Then will two at once woo one –
      That must needs be sport alone;
120   And those things do best please me
    That befall preposterously.
    Enter Lysander and Helena

LYSANDER

Why should you think that I should woo in scorn?
    Scorn and derision never come in tears.
Look when I vow, I weep; and vows so born,
    In their nativity all truth appears.
How can these things in me seem scorn to you,
Bearing the badge of faith to prove them true?

HELENA

You do advance your cunning more and more.
    When truth kills truth, O devilish-holy fray!
130 These vows are Hermia's. Will you give her o'er?
    Weigh oath with oath, and you will nothing weigh.
Your vows to her and me, put in two scales,
Will even weigh, and both as light as tales.

LYSANDER

I had no judgement when to her I swore.

HELENA

Nor none in my mind now you give her o'er.

LYSANDER

Demetrius loves her, and he loves not you.

DEMETRIUS (*wakes*)

O Helen, goddess, nymph, perfect, divine –
To what, my love, shall I compare thine eyne?
Crystal is muddy! O, how ripe in show
140 Thy lips – those kissing cherries – tempting grow!
That pure congealèd white, high Taurus' snow,
Fanned with the eastern wind, turns to a crow

When thou holdest up thy hand. O, let me kiss
This princess of pure white, this seal of bliss!

HELENA

O spite! O hell! I see you all are bent
To set against me for your merriment.
If you were civil and knew courtesy
You would not do me thus much injury.
Can you not hate me – as I know you do –
But you must join in souls to mock me too?   150
If you were men – as men you are in show –
You would not use a gentle lady so,
To vow, and swear, and superpraise my parts,
When, I am sure, you hate me with your hearts.
You both are rivals, and love Hermia;
And now both rivals to mock Helena.
A trim exploit, a manly enterprise –
To conjure tears up in a poor maid's eyes
With your derision. None of noble sort
Would so offend a virgin, and extort   160
A poor soul's patience, all to make you sport.

LYSANDER

You are unkind, Demetrius. Be not so,
For you love Hermia – this you know I know.
And hear: with all good will, with all my heart,
In Hermia's love I yield you up my part.
And yours of Helena to me bequeath,
Whom I do love, and will do to my death.

HELENA

Never did mockers waste more idle breath.

DEMETRIUS

Lysander, keep thy Hermia. I will none.
If e'er I loved her all that love is gone.   170
My heart to her but as guestwise sojourned,
And now to Helen is it home returned,
There to remain.

LYSANDER   Helen, it is not so.

DEMETRIUS

Disparage not the faith thou dost not know,
Lest to thy peril thou aby it dear.
Look where thy love comes: yonder is thy dear.

Enter Hermia

HERMIA

Dark night that from the eye his function takes
The ear more quick of apprehension makes.
Wherein it doth impair the seeing sense
180   It pays the hearing double recompense.
Thou art not by mine eye, Lysander, found;
Mine ear – I thank it – brought me to thy sound.
But why unkindly didst thou leave me so?

LYSANDER

Why should he stay whom love doth press to go?

HERMIA

What love could press Lysander from my side?

LYSANDER

Lysander's love, that would not let him bide:
Fair Helena, who more engilds the night
Than all yon fiery oes and eyes of light,
Why seekest thou me? Could not this make thee know
190   The hate I bare thee made me leave thee so?

HERMIA

You speak not as you think. It cannot be.

HELENA

Lo, she is one of this confederacy.
Now I perceive they have conjoined all three
To fashion this false sport in spite of me.
Injurious Hermia, most ungrateful maid,
Have you conspired, have you with these contrived
To bait me with this foul derision?
Is all the counsel that we two have shared –

The sisters' vows, the hours that we have spent
When we have chid the hasty-footed time   200
For parting us – O, is all forgot?
All schooldays' friendship, childhood innocence?
We, Hermia, like two artificial gods
Have with our needles created both one flower,
Both on one sampler, sitting on one cushion,
Both warbling of one song, both in one key,
As if our hands, our sides, voices, and minds
Had been incorporate. So we grew together
Like to a double cherry, seeming parted
But yet an union in partition,   210
Two lovely berries moulded on one stem,
So with two seeming bodies but one heart,
Two of the first, like coats in heraldry,
Due but to one, and crownèd with one crest.
And will you rent our ancient love asunder,
To join with men in scorning your poor friend?
It is not friendly, 'tis not maidenly.
Our sex as well as I may chide you for it,
Though I alone do feel the injury.

HERMIA

I am amazèd at your passionate words.   220
I scorn you not; it seems that you scorn me.

HELENA

Have you not set Lysander, as in scorn,
To follow me and praise my eyes and face?
And made your other love, Demetrius –
Who even but now did spurn me with his foot –
To call me goddess, nymph, divine and rare,
Precious, celestial? Wherefore speaks he this
To her he hates? And wherefore doth Lysander
Deny your love, so rich within his soul,
And tender me forsooth affection,   230

But by your setting on, by your consent?
What though I be not so in grace as you,
So hung upon with love, so fortunate,
But miserable most, to love unloved:
This you should pity rather than despise.

HERMIA

I understand not what you mean by this.

HELENA

Ay, do! Persever, counterfeit sad looks,
Make mouths upon me when I turn my back,
Wink each at other, hold the sweet jest up.
240   This sport well carried shall be chroniclèd.
If you have any pity, grace, or manners,
You would not make me such an argument.
But fare ye well. 'Tis partly my own fault,
Which death or absence soon shall remedy.

LYSANDER

Stay, gentle Helena, hear my excuse,
My love, my life, my soul, fair Helena!

HELENA

O, excellent!

HERMIA (*to Lysander*)
                Sweet, do not scorn her so.

DEMETRIUS

If she cannot entreat, I can compel.

LYSANDER

Thou canst compel no more than she entreat.
250   Thy threats have no more strength than her weak
        prayers.
Helen, I love thee. By my life, I do.
I swear by that which I will lose for thee
To prove him false that says I love thee not.

DEMETRIUS

I say I love thee more than he can do.

LYSANDER
  If thou say so, withdraw, and prove it too.
DEMETRIUS
  Quick, come.
HERMIA   Lysander, whereto tends all this?
LYSANDER
  Away, you Ethiope!
DEMETRIUS   No, no. He'll
  Seem to break loose, take on as he would follow,
  But yet come not. (*To Lysander*) You are a tame man, go.
LYSANDER
  Hang off, thou cat, thou burr! Vile thing, let loose,   260
  Or I will shake thee from me like a serpent.
HERMIA
  Why are you grown so rude? What change is this,
  Sweet love?
LYSANDER   Thy love? – out, tawny Tartar, out;
  Out, loathèd medicine! O hated potion, hence!
HERMIA
  Do you not jest?
HELENA   Yes, sooth, and so do you.
LYSANDER
  Demetrius, I will keep my word with thee.
DEMETRIUS
  I would I had your bond; for I perceive
  A weak bond holds you. I'll not trust your word.
LYSANDER
  What? Should I hurt her, strike her, kill her dead?
  Although I hate her, I'll not harm her so.   270
HERMIA
  What? Can you do me greater harm than hate?
  Hate me? Wherefore? O me, what news, my love?
  Am not I Hermia? Are not you Lysander?
  I am as fair now as I was erewhile.

Since night you loved me; yet since night you left me.
Why then, you left me – O, the gods forbid! –
In earnest, shall I say?

LYSANDER   Ay, by my life;
And never did desire to see thee more.
Therefore be out of hope, of question, of doubt,
Be certain. Nothing truer – 'tis no jest
That I do hate thee and love Helena.

HERMIA

O me, you juggler, you canker-blossom,
You thief of love! What, have you come by night
And stolen my love's heart from him?

HELENA   Fine, i'faith.
Have you no modesty, no maiden shame,
No touch of bashfulness? What, will you tear
Impatient answers from my gentle tongue?
Fie, fie, you counterfeit, you puppet, you!

HERMIA

Puppet? Why so? – Ay, that way goes the game.
Now I perceive that she hath made compare
Between our statures. She hath urged her height,
And with her personage, her tall personage,
Her height, forsooth, she hath prevailed with him.
And are you grown so high in his esteem
Because I am so dwarfish and so low?
How low am I, thou painted maypole? Speak!
How low am I? – I am not yet so low
But that my nails can reach unto thine eyes.

HELENA

I pray you, though you mock me, gentlemen,
Let her not hurt me. I was never curst.
I have no gift at all in shrewishness.
I am a right maid for my cowardice!
Let her not strike me. You perhaps may think

Because she is something lower than myself
That I can match her . . .

HERMIA   Lower? Hark, again!

HELENA

Good Hermia, do not be so bitter with me.
I evermore did love you, Hermia;
Did ever keep your counsels, never wronged you,
Save that in love unto Demetrius
I told him of your stealth unto this wood.   310
He followed you. For love I followed him.
But he hath chid me hence, and threatened me
To strike me, spurn me – nay, to kill me too.
And now, so you will let me quiet go,
To Athens will I bear my folly back
And follow you no further. Let me go.
You see how simple and how fond I am.

HERMIA

Why, get you gone! Who is't that hinders you?

HELENA

A foolish heart that I leave here behind.

HERMIA

What, with Lysander?

HELENA   With Demetrius.   320

LYSANDER

Be not afraid; she shall not harm thee, Helena.

DEMETRIUS

No, sir. She shall not, though you take her part.

HELENA

O, when she is angry she is keen and shrewd.
She was a vixen when she went to school,
And though she be but little, she is fierce.

HERMIA

Little again? Nothing but low and little?
Why will you suffer her to flout me thus?

Let me come to her.

LYSANDER   Get you gone, you dwarf,
You minimus of hindering knot-grass made,
330   You bead, you acorn.

DEMETRIUS   You are too officious
In her behalf that scorns your services.
Let her alone. Speak not of Helena,
Take not her part; for if thou dost intend
Never so little show of love to her,
Thou shalt aby it.

LYSANDER   Now she holds me not.
Now follow – if thou darest – to try whose right
Of thine or mine is most in Helena.

DEMETRIUS
Follow? Nay, I'll go with thee, cheek by jowl.
                              Exeunt Demetrius and Lysander

HERMIA
You, mistress – all this coil is 'long of you.
340   Nay – go not back.

HELENA   I will not trust you, I,
Nor longer stay in your curst company.
Your hands than mine are quicker for a fray.
My legs are longer, though, to run away!   *Exit*

HERMIA
I am amazed, and know not what to say!   *Exit*
    Oberon and Puck come forward

OBERON
This is thy negligence. Still thou mistakest,
Or else committest thy knaveries wilfully.

PUCK
Believe me, King of shadows, I mistook.
Did not you tell me I should know the man
By the Athenian garments he had on?

And so far blameless proves my enterprise   350
That I have 'nointed an Athenian's eyes.
And so far am I glad it so did sort,
As this their jangling I esteem a sport.

OBERON

Thou seest these lovers seek a place to fight.
Hie therefore, Robin, overcast the night.
The starry welkin cover thou anon
With drooping fog as black as Acheron,
And lead these testy rivals so astray
As one come not within another's way.
Like to Lysander sometime frame thy tongue,   360
Then stir Demetrius up with bitter wrong,
And sometime rail thou like Demetrius;
And from each other look thou lead them thus
Till o'er their brows death-counterfeiting sleep
With leaden legs and batty wings doth creep.
Then crush this herb into Lysander's eye —
Whose liquor hath this virtuous property,
To take from thence all error with his might,
And make his eyeballs roll with wonted sight.
When they next wake, all this derision   370
Shall seem a dream and fruitless vision,
And back to Athens shall the lovers wend
With league whose date till death shall never end.
Whiles I in this affair do thee employ
I'll to my Queen and beg her Indian boy,
And then I will her charmèd eye release
From monster's view, and all things shall be peace.

PUCK

My fairy lord, this must be done with haste,
For night's swift dragons cut the clouds full fast,
And yonder shines Aurora's harbinger,   380
At whose approach ghosts wandering here and there

Troop home to churchyards. Damnèd spirits all
That in crossways and floods have burial
Already to their wormy beds are gone.
For fear lest day should look their shames upon
They wilfully themselves exile from light,
And must for aye consort with black-browed night.

OBERON

But we are spirits of another sort.
I with the morning's love have oft made sport,
And like a forester the groves may tread
Even till the eastern gate all fiery red
Opening on Neptune with fair blessèd beams
Turns into yellow gold his salt green streams.
But notwithstanding, haste, make no delay;
We may effect this business yet ere day.   *Exit*

PUCK

Up and down, up and down,
I will lead them up and down.
I am feared in field and town.
Goblin, lead them up and down.
Here comes one.
          Enter Lysander

LYSANDER

Where art thou, proud Demetrius? Speak thou now.

PUCK (*in Demetrius' voice*)

Here, villain, drawn and ready! Where art thou?

LYSANDER

I will be with thee straight.

PUCK (*in Demetrius' voice*)   Follow me then
To plainer ground.   *Exit Lysander*
          Enter Demetrius

DEMETRIUS   Lysander, speak again.
Thou runaway, thou coward – art thou fled?
Speak. In some bush? Where dost thou hide thy head?

PUCK (*in Lysander's voice*)
    Thou coward, art thou bragging to the stars,
    Telling the bushes that thou lookest for wars,
    And wilt not come? Come, recreant. Come, thou child,
    I'll whip thee with a rod. He is defiled   410
    That draws a sword on thee.

DEMETRIUS   Yea, art thou there?

PUCK (*in Lysander's voice*)
    Follow my voice. We'll try no manhood here.

                  Exeunt Puck and Demetrius

    Enter Lysander

LYSANDER
    He goes before me, and still dares me on;
    When I come where he calls, then he is gone.
    The villain is much lighter-heeled than I.
    I followed fast, but faster he did fly,
    That fallen am I in dark uneven way,
    And here will rest me. (*He lies down*) Come, thou gentle
        day,
    For if but once thou show me thy grey light
    I'll find Demetrius and revenge this spite.   420

    He sleeps

    Enter Puck and Demetrius

PUCK (*in Lysander's voice*)
    Ho, ho, ho, coward! Why comest thou not?

DEMETRIUS
    Abide me if thou darest, for well I wot
    Thou runnest before me, shifting every place,
    And darest not stand nor look me in the face.
    Where art thou now?

PUCK (*in Lysander's voice*)
               Come hither; I am here.

DEMETRIUS
    Nay, then thou mockest me. Thou shalt buy this dear

If ever I thy face by daylight see.
Now, go thy way. Faintness constraineth me
To measure out my length on this cold bed.
430   By day's approach look to be visited.
        He lies down and sleeps
        Enter Helena

HELENA
   O weary night! O long and tedious night,
        Abate thy hours, shine comforts from the East,
   That I may back to Athens by daylight
        From these that my poor company detest.
   And sleep, that sometimes shuts up sorrow's eye,
   Steal me awhile from mine own company.
        She lies down and sleeps

PUCK
        Yet but three? Come one more,
        Two of both kinds makes up four.
        Here she comes, curst and sad.
440   Cupid is a knavish lad
        Thus to make poor females mad.
        Enter Hermia

HERMIA
   Never so weary, never so in woe,
        Bedabbled with the dew, and torn with briars –
   I can no further crawl, no further go.
        My legs can keep no pace with my desires.
   Here will I rest me till the break of day.
   Heavens shield Lysander, if they mean a fray.
        She lies down and sleeps

PUCK
                        On the ground
                        Sleep sound.
                        I'll apply
450   To your eye,

Gentle lover, remedy.

He squeezes the juice on Lysander's eyes

When thou wakest,

Thou takest

True delight

In the sight

Of thy former lady's eye.

And the country proverb known,

That every man should take his own,

In your waking shall be shown.   460

Jack shall have Jill;

Naught shall go ill.

The man shall have his mare again, and all shall be well.

Exit

*

Enter Titania, and Bottom, and Fairies; and Oberon **IV.1**
behind them

TITANIA

Come, sit thee down upon this flowery bed
    While I thy amiable cheeks do coy,
And stick muskroses in thy sleek, smooth head,
    And kiss thy fair large ears, my gentle joy.

BOTTOM Where's Peaseblossom?

PEASEBLOSSOM Ready.

BOTTOM Scratch my head, Peaseblossom. Where's
Monsieur Cobweb?

COBWEB Ready.

BOTTOM Monsieur Cobweb, good Monsieur, get you your   10
weapons in your hand and kill me a red-hipped humble
bee on the top of a thistle; and, good Monsieur, bring
me the honey bag. Do not fret yourself too much in the

action, Monsieur; and, good Monsieur, have a care the
honey bag break not, I would be loath to have you over-
flown with a honey bag, signor. Where's Monsieur
Mustardseed?

MUSTARDSEED Ready.

BOTTOM Give me your neaf, Monsieur Mustardseed.
20   Pray you, leave your courtesy, good Monsieur.

MUSTARDSEED What's your will?

BOTTOM Nothing, good Monsieur, but to help Cavalery
Cobweb to scratch. I must to the barber's, Monsieur,
for methinks I am marvellous hairy about the face. And
I am such a tender ass, if my hair do but tickle me, I
must scratch.

TITANIA
What, wilt thou hear some music, my sweet love?

BOTTOM I have a reasonable good ear in music. Let's have
the tongs and the bones.

TITANIA
30   Or say, sweet love, what thou desirest to eat.

BOTTOM Truly, a peck of provender. I could munch your
good dry oats. Methinks I have a great desire to a bottle
of hay. Good hay, sweet hay hath no fellow.

TITANIA
I have a venturous fairy that shall seek
The squirrel's hoard, and fetch thee new nuts.

BOTTOM I had rather have a handful or two of dried pease.
But, I pray you, let none of your people stir me. I have
an exposition of sleep come upon me.

TITANIA
Sleep thou, and I will wind thee in my arms.
40   Fairies be gone, and be all ways away.   *Exeunt Fairies*
So doth the woodbine the sweet honeysuckle
Gently entwist; the female ivy so
Enrings the barky fingers of the elm.

O, how I love thee! How I dote on thee!
They sleep. Enter Puck

OBERON (*comes forward*)
Welcome, good Robin. Seest thou this sweet sight?
Her dotage now I do begin to pity.
For, meeting her of late behind the wood
Seeking sweet favours for this hateful fool,
I did upbraid her and fall out with her,
For she his hairy temples then had rounded   50
With coronet of fresh and fragrant flowers.
And that same dew which sometime on the buds
Was wont to swell, like round and orient pearls,
Stood now within the pretty flowerets' eyes
Like tears that did their own disgrace bewail.
When I had at my pleasure taunted her,
And she in mild terms begged my patience,
I then did ask of her her changeling child,
Which straight she gave me, and her fairy sent
To bear him to my bower in Fairyland.   60
And now I have the boy I will undo
This hateful imperfection of her eyes.
And, gentle Puck, take this transformèd scalp
From off the head of this Athenian swain,
That, he awaking when the other do,
May all to Athens back again repair
And think no more of this night's accidents
But as the fierce vexation of a dream.
But first I will release the Fairy Queen.
    (*To Titania*)
    Be as thou wast wont to be;   70
    See as thou wast wont to see.
    Dian's bud o'er Cupid's flower
    Hath such force and blessèd power.
Now, my Titania, wake you, my sweet Queen!

TITANIA (*wakes*)
  My Oberon, what visions have I seen!
  Methought I was enamoured of an ass.

OBERON
  There lies your love.

TITANIA   How came these things to pass?
  O, how mine eyes do loathe his visage now!

OBERON
  Silence awhile! Robin, take off this head.
80 Titania, music call, and strike more dead
  Than common sleep of all these five the sense.

TITANIA
  Music, ho! Music such as charmeth sleep.

PUCK (*to Bottom, removing the ass's head*)
  Now when thou wakest with thine own fool's eyes peep.

OBERON
  Sound, music! (*Music*) Come, my Queen, take hands
      with me,
  And rock the ground whereon these sleepers be.
      They dance
  Now thou and I are new in amity,
  And will tomorrow midnight solemnly
  Dance in Duke Theseus' house triumphantly,
  And bless it to all fair prosperity.
90 There shall the pairs of faithful lovers be
  Wedded with Theseus all in jollity.

PUCK
    Fairy king, attend, and mark:
    I do hear the morning lark.

OBERON
    Then, my queen, in silence sad,
    Trip we after night's shade.
    We the globe can compass soon,
    Swifter than the wandering moon.

TITANIA

    Come, my lord, and in our flight
    Tell me how it came this night
    That I sleeping here was found   100
    With these mortals on the ground.

              Exeunt Oberon, Titania, and Puck
    Horns sound. Enter Theseus with Hippolyta, Egeus,
    and all his train

THESEUS

    Go, one of you; find out the forester;
    For now our observation is performed.
    And since we have the vaward of the day,
    My love shall hear the music of my hounds.
    Uncouple in the western valley; let them go.
    Dispatch, I say, and find the forester. *Exit an attendant*
    We will, fair Queen, up to the mountain's top,
    And mark the musical confusion
    Of hounds and echo in conjunction.   110

HIPPOLYTA

    I was with Hercules and Cadmus once,
    When in a wood of Crete they bayed the bear
    With hounds of Sparta. Never did I hear
    Such gallant chiding, for besides the groves,
    The skies, the fountains, every region near
    Seemed all one mutual cry. I never heard
    So musical a discord, such sweet thunder.

THESEUS

    My hounds are bred out of the Spartan kind;
    So flewed, so sanded; and their heads are hung
    With ears that sweep away the morning dew;   120
    Crook-kneed; and dewlapped like Thessalian bulls;
    Slow in pursuit, but matched in mouth like bells,
    Each under each. A cry more tuneable
    Was never hallooed to nor cheered with horn

In Crete, in Sparta, nor in Thessaly.
Judge when you hear.

He sees the sleepers

But soft, what nymphs are these?

EGEUS

My lord, this is my daughter here asleep,
And this Lysander; this Demetrius is,
This Helena – old Nedar's Helena.
130   I wonder of their being here together.

THESEUS

No doubt they rose up early to observe
The rite of May, and hearing our intent
Came here in grace of our solemnity.
But speak, Egeus: is not this the day
That Hermia should give answer of her choice?

EGEUS   It is, my lord.

THESEUS

Go, bid the huntsmen wake them with their horns.

*Horns sound; the lovers wake; shout within; the
lovers start up*

Good morrow, friends – Saint Valentine is past!
Begin these woodbirds but to couple now?

LYSANDER

140   Pardon, my lord.

THESEUS   I pray you all, stand up.
I know you two are rival enemies.
How comes this gentle concord in the world,
That hatred is so far from jealousy
To sleep by hate, and fear no enmity?

LYSANDER

My lord, I shall reply amazedly,
Half sleep, half waking. But as yet, I swear,
I cannot truly say how I came here.
But as I think – for truly would I speak –

And now I do bethink me, so it is:
I came with Hermia hither. Our intent   150
Was to be gone from Athens where we might
Without the peril of the Athenian law . . .

EGEUS

Enough, enough – my lord, you have enough!
I beg the law, the law upon his head.
They would have stolen away, they would, Demetrius,
Thereby to have defeated you and me –
You of your wife, and me of my consent –
Of my consent that she should be your wife.

DEMETRIUS

My lord, fair Helen told me of their stealth,
Of this their purpose hither to this wood,   160
And I in fury hither followed them,
Fair Helena in fancy following me.
But, my good lord – I wot not by what power,
But by some power it is – my love to Hermia,
Melted as the snow, seems to me now
As the remembrance of an idle gaud
Which in my childhood I did dote upon;
And all the faith, the virtue of my heart,
The object and the pleasure of mine eye,
Is only Helena. To her, my lord,   170
Was I betrothed ere I saw Hermia;
But like a sickness did I loathe this food.
But, as in health come to my natural taste,
Now I do wish it, love it, long for it,
And will for evermore be true to it.

THESEUS

Fair lovers, you are fortunately met.
Of this discourse we more will hear anon.
Egeus, I will overbear your will;
For in the temple by and by with us

180 These couples shall eternally be knit.
And – for the morning now is something worn –
Our purposed hunting shall be set aside.
Away with us to Athens. Three and three,
We'll hold a feast in great solemnity.
Come, Hippolyta.

Exit Theseus with Hippolyta, Egeus, and his train

DEMETRIUS

These things seem small and undistinguishable,
Like far-off mountains turnèd into clouds.

HERMIA

Methinks I see these things with parted eye,
When everything seems double.

HELENA   So methinks,
190 And I have found Demetrius, like a jewel,
Mine own and not mine own.

DEMETRIUS   Are you sure
That we are awake? It seems to me
That yet we sleep, we dream. Do not you think
The Duke was here, and bid us follow him?

HERMIA

Yea, and my father.

HELENA   And Hippolyta.

LYSANDER

And he did bid us follow to the temple.

DEMETRIUS

Why, then, we are awake. Let's follow him,
And by the way let's recount our dreams.

Exeunt Demetrius, Helena, Lysander, and Hermia
Bottom wakes

BOTTOM When my cue comes, call me, and I will answer.
200 My next is 'Most fair Pyramus'. Heigh ho! Peter
Quince! Flute the bellows-mender! Snout the tinker!
Starveling! God's my life – stolen hence and left me

asleep! – I have had a most rare vision. I have had a
dream past the wit of man to say what dream it was. Man
is but an ass if he go about to expound this dream. Methought I was – there is no man can tell what. Methought
I was – and methought I had – but man is but a patched
fool if he will offer to say what methought I had. The
eye of man hath not heard, the ear of man hath not seen,
man's hand is not able to taste, his tongue to conceive,   210
nor his heart to report what my dream was! I will get
Peter Quince to write a ballad of this dream. It shall be
called 'Bottom's Dream', because it hath no bottom; and
I will sing it in the latter end of a play before the Duke.
Peradventure, to make it the more gracious, I shall sing
it at her death.

> *Exit*

Enter Quince, Flute, Snout, and Starveling   IV.2

QUINCE Have you sent to Bottom's house? Is he come
home yet?

STARVELING He cannot be heard of. Out of doubt he is
transported.

FLUTE If he come not, then the play is marred. It goes not
forward. Doth it?

QUINCE It is not possible. You have not a man in all
Athens able to discharge Pyramus but he.

FLUTE No, he hath simply the best wit of any handicraft
man in Athens.   10

QUINCE Yea, and the best person, too; and he is a very
paramour for a sweet voice.

FLUTE You must say 'paragon'. A paramour is – God bless
us – a thing of naught.

Enter Snug the joiner

SNUG Masters, the Duke is coming from the temple, and

there is two or three lords and ladies more married. If
our sport had gone forward, we had all been made men.

FLUTE O, sweet Bully Bottom! Thus hath he lost sixpence
a day during his life. He could not have scaped sixpence
a day. An the Duke had not given him sixpence a day for
playing Pyramus, I'll be hanged. He would have de-
served it. Sixpence a day in Pyramus, or nothing.

Enter Bottom

BOTTOM Where are these lads? Where are these hearts?

QUINCE Bottom! O most courageous day! O most happy
hour!

BOTTOM Masters, I am to discourse wonders – but ask me
not what; for if I tell you, I am not true Athenian. – I
will tell you everything, right as it fell out!

QUINCE Let us hear, sweet Bottom!

BOTTOM Not a word of me! All that I will tell you is – that
the Duke hath dined. Get your apparel together, good
strings to your beards, new ribbons to your pumps.
Meet presently at the palace. Every man look o'er his
part. For the short and the long is, our play is preferred.
In any case, let Thisbe have clean linen; and let not him
that plays the lion pare his nails, for they shall hang out
for the lion's claws. And, most dear actors, eat no onions
nor garlic; for we are to utter sweet breath, and I do
not doubt but to hear them say it is a sweet comedy. No
more words. Away – go, away!

Exeunt Bottom and his fellows

*

Enter Theseus, Hippolyta, Philostrate, lords, and   V.I
attendants

HIPPOLYTA

'Tis strange, my Theseus, that these lovers speak of.

THESEUS

More strange than true. I never may believe
These antique fables, nor these fairy toys.
Lovers and madmen have such seething brains,
Such shaping fantasies, that apprehend
More than cool reason ever comprehends.
The lunatic, the lover, and the poet
Are of imagination all compact.
One sees more devils than vast hell can hold.
That is the madman. The lover, all as frantic,   10
Sees Helen's beauty in a brow of Egypt.
The poet's eye, in a fine frenzy rolling,
Doth glance from heaven to earth, from earth to heaven.
And as imagination bodies forth
The forms of things unknown, the poet's pen
Turns them to shapes, and gives to airy nothing
A local habitation and a name.
Such tricks hath strong imagination
That if it would but apprehend some joy,
It comprehends some bringer of that joy.   20
Or in the night, imagining some fear,
How easy is a bush supposed a bear?

HIPPOLYTA

But all the story of the night told over,
And all their minds transfigured so together,
More witnesseth than fancy's images,
And grows to something of great constancy;
But howsoever, strange and admirable.

Enter the lovers: Lysander, Demetrius, Hermia, and
Helena

THESEUS
    Here come the lovers, full of joy and mirth.
    Joy, gentle friends, joy and fresh days of love
30   Accompany your hearts.

LYSANDER   More than to us
    Wait in your royal walks, your board, your bed.

THESEUS
    Come now, what masques, what dances shall we have
    To wear away this long age of three hours
    Between our after-supper and bedtime?
    Where is our usual manager of mirth?
    What revels are in hand? Is there no play
    To ease the anguish of a torturing hour?
    Call Philostrate.

PHILOSTRATE   Here, mighty Theseus.

THESEUS
    Say, what abridgement have you for this evening?
40   What masque, what music? How shall we beguile
    The lazy time if not with some delight?

PHILOSTRATE (*giving a paper*)
    There is a brief how many sports are ripe.
    Make choice of which your highness will see first.

THESEUS
    The Battle with the Centaurs, 'to be sung
    By an Athenian eunuch to the harp'.
    We'll none of that. That have I told my love
    In glory of my kinsman, Hercules.
    The riot of the tipsy Bacchanals,
    Tearing the Thracian singer in their rage.
50   That is an old device, and it was played
    When I from Thebes came last a conqueror.
    The thrice three Muses mourning for the death
    Of learning, late deceased in beggary.
    That is some satire keen and critical,

Not sorting with a nuptial ceremony.
A tedious brief scene of young Pyramus
And his love Thisbe; 'very tragical mirth'.
Merry and tragical? Tedious and brief?
That is, hot ice and wondrous strange snow.
How shall we find the concord of this discord?   60

PHILOSTRATE
A play there is, my lord, some ten words long,
Which is as 'brief' as I have known a play.
But by ten words, my lord, it is too long,
Which makes it 'tedious'. For in all the play
There is not one word apt, one player fitted.
And 'tragical', my noble lord, it is,
For Pyramus therein doth kill himself,
Which when I saw rehearsed, I must confess,
Made mine eyes water: but more 'merry' tears
The passion of loud laughter never shed.   70

THESEUS
What are they that do play it?

PHILOSTRATE
Hard-handed men that work in Athens here,
Which never laboured in their minds till now,
And now have toiled their unbreathed memories
With this same play against your nuptial.

THESEUS
And we will hear it.

PHILOSTRATE   No, my noble lord,
It is not for you. I have heard it over,
And it is nothing, nothing in the world,
Unless you can find sport in their intents,
Extremely stretched, and conned with cruel pain,   80
To do you service.

THESEUS   I will hear that play,
For never anything can be amiss

When simpleness and duty tender it.
Go bring them in; and take your places, ladies.

Exit Philostrate

HIPPOLYTA

I love not to see wretchedness o'ercharged,
And duty in his service perishing.

THESEUS

Why, gentle sweet, you shall see no such thing.

HIPPOLYTA

He says they can do nothing in this kind.

THESEUS

The kinder we, to give them thanks for nothing.
90   Our sport shall be to take what they mistake;
And what poor duty cannot do, noble respect
Takes it in might, not merit.
Where I have come, great clerks have purposèd
To greet me with premeditated welcomes,
Where I have seen them shiver and look pale,
Make periods in the midst of sentences,
Throttle their practised accent in their fears,
And in conclusion dumbly have broke off,
Not paying me a welcome. Trust me, sweet,
100   Out of this silence yet I picked a welcome,
And in the modesty of fearful duty
I read as much as from the rattling tongue
Of saucy and audacious eloquence.
Love, therefore, and tongue-tied simplicity
In least speak most, to my capacity.

Enter Philostrate

PHILOSTRATE

So please your grace, the Prologue is addressed.

THESEUS Let him approach.

Flourish of trumpets
Enter Quince as Prologue

QUINCE

If we offend it is with our good will.
That you should think we come not to offend
But with good will. To show our simple skill,   110
That is the true beginning of our end.
Consider then we come but in despite.
We do not come as minding to content you,
Our true intent is. All for your delight
We are not here. That you should here repent you
The actors are at hand, and by their show
You shall know all that you are like to know.

THESEUS This fellow doth not stand upon points.

LYSANDER He hath rid his prologue like a rough colt; he
knows not the stop. A good moral, my lord: it is not   120
enough to speak, but to speak true.

HIPPOLYTA Indeed, he hath played on his prologue like a
child on a recorder – a sound, but not in government.

THESEUS His speech was like a tangled chain: nothing
impaired, but all disordered. Who is next?

*Enter Bottom as Pyramus, Flute as Thisbe, Snout as
Wall, Starveling as Moonshine, and Snug as Lion,
a trumpeter before them*

QUINCE

Gentles, perchance you wonder at this show;
But wonder on, till truth make all things plain.
This man is Pyramus, if you would know;
This beauteous lady Thisbe is, certain.
This man with lime and roughcast doth present   130
Wall – that vile wall which did these lovers sunder;
And through Wall's chink, poor souls, they are content
To whisper. At the which let no man wonder.
This man with lantern, dog, and bush of thorn
Presenteth Moonshine. For if you will know
By moonshine did these lovers think no scorn

　　　To meet at Ninus' tomb, there, there to woo.
　　　This grisly beast — which Lion hight by name —
　　　The trusty Thisbe coming first by night
140　　Did scare away, or rather did affright.
　　　And as she fled, her mantle she did fall,
　　　　Which Lion vile with bloody mouth did stain.
　　　Anon comes Pyramus — sweet youth and tall —
　　　　And finds his trusty Thisbe's mantle slain.
　　　Whereat with blade — with bloody, blameful blade —
　　　　He bravely broached his boiling bloody breast.
　　　And Thisbe, tarrying in mulberry shade,
　　　　His dagger drew, and died. For all the rest,
　　　Let Lion, Moonshine, Wall, and lovers twain
150　　At large discourse while here they do remain.

　　　　　Exeunt Quince, Bottom, Flute, Snug, and Starveling
THESEUS I wonder if the lion be to speak.
DEMETRIUS
　　　No wonder, my lord — one lion may, when many asses do.
SNOUT *as Wall*
　　　In this same interlude it doth befall
　　　That I — one Snout by name — present a wall.
　　　And such a wall as I would have you think
　　　That had in it a crannied hole or chink,
　　　Through which the lovers, Pyramus and Thisbe,
　　　Did whisper often, very secretly.
　　　This loam, this roughcast, and this stone doth show
　　　That I am that same wall; the truth is so.
160　　And this the cranny is, right and sinister,
　　　Through which the fearful lovers are to whisper.
THESEUS Would you desire lime and hair to speak better?
DEMETRIUS It is the wittiest partition that ever I heard
　　　discourse, my lord.

　　　　Enter Bottom as Pyramus

THESEUS Pyramus draws near the wall. Silence!

BOTTOM *as Pyramus*

  O grim-looked night, O night with hue so black,

    O night which ever art when day is not!

  O night, O night, alack, alack, alack,

    I fear my Thisbe's promise is forgot.   170

  And thou, O wall, O sweet, O lovely wall,

    That standest between her father's ground and mine,

  Thou wall, O wall, O sweet and lovely wall,

    Show me thy chink to blink through with mine eyne.

    Wall holds up his fingers

  Thanks, courteous wall; Jove shield thee well for this.

    But what see I? No Thisbe do I see.

  O wicked wall, through whom I see no bliss:

    Cursed be thy stones for thus deceiving me!

THESEUS The wall, methinks, being sensible, should curse

  again.   180

BOTTOM No, in truth sir, he should not. 'Deceiving me' is

  Thisbe's cue. She is to enter now, and I am to spy her

  through the wall. You shall see – it will fall pat as I told

  you. Yonder she comes.

    Enter Flute as Thisbe

FLUTE *as Thisbe*

  O wall, full often hast thou heard my moans

    For parting my fair Pyramus and me.

  My cherry lips have often kissed thy stones,

    Thy stones with lime and hair knit up in thee.

BOTTOM *as Pyramus*

  I see a voice. Now will I to the chink

    To spy an I can hear my Thisbe's face.   190

  Thisbe!

FLUTE *as Thisbe*

      My love! Thou art my love, I think?

BOTTOM *as Pyramus*

> Think what thou wilt, I am thy lover's grace,
> And like Limander am I trusty still.

FLUTE *as Thisbe*

> And I like Helen till the Fates me kill.

BOTTOM *as Pyramus*

> Not Shafalus to Procrus was so true.

FLUTE *as Thisbe*

> As Shafalus to Procrus, I to you.

BOTTOM *as Pyramus*

> O, kiss me through the hole of this vile wall!

FLUTE *as Thisbe*

> I kiss the wall's hole, not your lips at all.

BOTTOM *as Pyramus*

> Wilt thou at Ninny's tomb meet me straight way?

FLUTE *as Thisbe*

200   Tide life, tide death, I come without delay.

Exeunt Bottom and Flute

SNOUT *as Wall*

> Thus have I, Wall, my part dischargèd so;
> And being done, thus Wall away doth go.   *Exit*

THESEUS Now is the mural down between the two neighbours.

DEMETRIUS No remedy, my lord, when walls are so wilful to hear without warning.

HIPPOLYTA This is the silliest stuff that ever I heard.

THESEUS The best in this kind are but shadows; and the worst are no worse, if imagination amend them.

210 HIPPOLYTA It must be your imagination, then, and not theirs.

THESEUS If we imagine no worse of them than they of themselves, they may pass for excellent men. Here come two noble beasts in: a man and a lion.

Enter Snug as Lion and Starveling as Moonshine

SNUG *as Lion*

> You, ladies – you whose gentle hearts do fear
>> The smallest monstrous mouse that creeps on floor –
> May now, perchance, both quake and tremble here,
>> When Lion rough in wildest rage doth roar.
> Then know that I as Snug the joiner am
> A lion fell, nor else no lion's dam,   220
> For if I should as lion come in strife
> Into this place, 'twere pity on my life.

THESEUS A very gentle beast, and of a good conscience.

DEMETRIUS The very best at a beast, my lord, that e'er I saw.

LYSANDER This lion is a very fox for his valour.

THESEUS True; and a goose for his discretion.

DEMETRIUS Not so, my lord; for his valour cannot carry his discretion; and the fox carries the goose.

THESEUS His discretion, I am sure, cannot carry his   230
valour; for the goose carries not the fox. It is well: leave it to his discretion, and let us listen to the moon.

STARVELING *as Moonshine*

> This lanthorn doth the hornèd moon present.

DEMETRIUS He should have worn the horns on his head.

THESEUS He is no crescent, and his horns are invisible within the circumference.

STARVELING *as Moonshine*

> This lanthorn doth the hornèd moon present;
>> Myself the man i'th'moon do seem to be.

THESEUS This is the greatest error of all the rest; the man should be put into the lantern. How is it else the man   240
i'th'moon?

DEMETRIUS He dares not come there, for the candle. For, you see, it is already in snuff.

HIPPOLYTA I am aweary of this moon. Would he would change.

THESEUS It appears by his small light of discretion that
he is in the wane. But yet in courtesy, in all reason, we
must stay the time.

LYSANDER Proceed, Moon.

250 STARVELING All that I have to say is to tell you that the
lantern is the moon, I the man i'th'moon, this thorn
bush my thorn bush, and this dog my dog.

DEMETRIUS Why, all these should be in the lantern; for
all these are in the moon. But silence: here comes Thisbe.

Enter Flute as Thisbe

FLUTE *as Thisbe*
This is old Ninny's tomb. Where is my love?

SNUG *as Lion*
O!

Lion roars. Flute as Thisbe runs off

DEMETRIUS Well roared, Lion!

THESEUS Well run, Thisbe!

HIPPOLYTA Well shone, Moon! Truly, the moon shines
260   with a good grace.

Lion tears Thisbe's mantle. Exit

THESEUS Well moused, Lion!

DEMETRIUS And then came Pyramus.

LYSANDER And so the lion vanished.

Enter Bottom as Pyramus

BOTTOM *as Pyramus*
Sweet moon, I thank thee for thy sunny beams;
    I thank thee, moon, for shining now so bright;
For by thy gracious, golden, glittering beams
    I trust to take of truest Thisbe sight.
                But stay – O spite!
                But mark, poor Knight,
270   What dreadful dole is here?
                Eyes, do you see? –
                How can it be?

O dainty duck, O dear!

Thy mantle good –

What, stained with blood!

Approach, ye Furies fell.

O Fates, come, come,

Cut thread and thrum,

Quail, crush, conclude, and quell.

THESEUS This passion, and the death of a dear friend,   280
would go near to make a man look sad.

HIPPOLYTA Beshrew my heart, but I pity the man.

BOTTOM *as Pyramus*

O wherefore, nature, didst thou lions frame,
  Since lion vile hath here deflowered my dear?
Which is – no, no, which was – the fairest dame
  That lived, that loved, that liked, that looked with cheer.

Come tears, confound;

Out sword, and wound

The pap of Pyramus.

Ay, that left pap,   290

Where heart doth hop.

Thus die I – thus, thus, thus.

He stabs himself

Now am I dead,

Now am I fled;

My soul is in the sky.

Tongue, lose thy light;

Moon, take thy flight;

                  Exit Starveling as Moonshine

Now die, die, die, die, die.   *He dies*

DEMETRIUS No die, but an ace for him; for he is but one.

LYSANDER Less than an ace, man; for he is dead. He is   300
nothing.

THESEUS With the help of a surgeon he might yet recover,
and prove an ass.

HIPPOLYTA How chance Moonshine is gone before
    Thisbe comes back and finds her lover?

THESEUS She will find him by starlight. Here she comes;
    and her passion ends the play.

    Enter Flute as Thisbe

HIPPOLYTA Methinks she should not use a long one for
    such a Pyramus. I hope she will be brief.

310 DEMETRIUS A mote will turn the balance which Pyramus,
    which Thisbe is the better – he for a man, God warrant
    us; she for a woman, God bless us.

LYSANDER She hath spied him already, with those sweet
    eyes.

DEMETRIUS And thus she means, videlicet:

FLUTE *as Thisbe*

        Asleep, my love?

        What, dead, my dove?

    O Pyramus, arise.

        Speak, speak. Quite dumb?

320   Dead, dead? A tomb

    Must cover thy sweet eyes.

        These lily lips,

        This cherry nose,

    These yellow cowslip cheeks

        Are gone, are gone.

        Lovers, make moan –

    His eyes were green as leeks.

        O sisters three,

        Come, come to me

330   With hands as pale as milk;

        Lay them in gore,

        Since you have shore

    With shears his thread of silk.

        Tongue, not a word!

        Come, trusty sword,

Come blade, my breast imbrue.

She stabs herself

And farewell friends.

Thus Thisbe ends.

Adieu, adieu, adieu!

She dies

THESEUS Moonshine and Lion are left to bury the dead.   340

DEMETRIUS Ay, and Wall, too.

BOTTOM (*starting up*) No, I assure you, the wall is down that parted their fathers. Will it please you to see the epilogue, or to hear a Bergomask dance between two of our company?

THESEUS No epilogue, I pray you; for your play needs no excuse. Never excuse; for when the players are all dead, there need none to be blamed. Marry, if he that writ it had played Pyramus and hanged himself in Thisbe's garter, it would have been a fine tragedy. And so it is,   350 truly, and very notably discharged. But come, your Bergomask; let your epilogue alone.

A dance. Exeunt Bottom and his fellows

The iron tongue of midnight hath told twelve.

Lovers, to bed; 'tis almost fairy time.

I fear we shall outsleep the coming morn

As much as we this night have overwatched.

This palpable-gross play hath well beguiled

The heavy gait of night. Sweet friends, to bed.

A fortnight hold we this solemnity

In nightly revels and new jollity.   360

Exeunt Theseus, Hippolyta, Philostrate,
Demetrius, Helena, Lysander, Hermia,
lords, and attendants

Enter Puck

PUCK

Now the hungry lion roars

And the wolf behowls the moon,
Whilst the heavy ploughman snores
   All with weary task foredone.
Now the wasted brands do glow
   Whilst the screech-owl, screeching loud,
Puts the wretch that lies in woe
   In remembrance of a shroud.
Now it is the time of night
370   That the graves, all gaping wide,
Every one lets forth his sprite
   In the churchway paths to glide.
And we fairies, that do run
   By the triple Hecate's team,
From the presence of the sun
   Following darkness like a dream,
Now are frolic. Not a mouse
Shall disturb this hallowed house.
I am sent with broom before
380 To sweep the dust behind the door.
Enter Oberon and Titania, with all their train

OBERON

Through the house give glimmering light
   By the dead and drowsy fire;
Every elf and fairy sprite
   Hop as light as bird from briar,
And this ditty after me
Sing, and dance it trippingly.

TITANIA

First rehearse your song by rote,
To each word a warbling note.
Hand in hand with fairy grace
390 Will we sing and bless this place.
Song and dance

OBERON

    Now until the break of day
    Through this house each fairy stray.
    To the best bride bed will we,
    Which by us shall blessèd be;
    And the issue there create
    Ever shall be fortunate.
    So shall all the couples three
    Ever true in loving be,
    And the blots of nature's hand
    Shall not in their issue stand.   400
    Never mole, harelip, nor scar,
    Nor mark prodigious, such as are
    Despisèd in nativity,
    Shall upon their children be.
    With this field dew consecrate
    Every fairy take his gait,
    And each several chamber bless
    Through this palace with sweet peace;
    And the owner of it blessed
    Ever shall in safety rest.   410
    Trip away; make no stay.
    Meet me all by break of day.

        Exeunt Oberon, Titania, and their train

PUCK (*to the audience*)

    If we shadows have offended,
    Think but this, and all is mended:
    That you have but slumbered here
    While these visions did appear.
    And this weak and idle theme,
    No more yielding but a dream,
    Gentles, do not reprehend.
    If you pardon, we will mend.   420
    And, as I am an honest Puck,

If we have unearnèd luck
Now to scape the serpent's tongue
We will make amends ere long,
Else the Puck a liar call.
So, good night unto you all.
Give me your hands if we be friends,
And Robin shall restore amends.   *Exit*

An Account of the Text

A Midsummer Night's Dream was first published by Thomas Fisher in 1600 in an edition believed to have been printed from a manuscript written by Shakespeare himself. This edition is known as the first Quarto. It was reprinted in 1619 in an edition falsely dated 1600; this is the second Quarto, a reprint of the first, with only minor differences. The play was also included in the collected edition of Shakespeare's plays published in 1623, known as the first Folio. Here it appears to have been printed from a copy of the second Quarto in which some alterations had been made from a theatrical copy. The alterations correct some errors in the original text, and add some information about its staging.

The edition closest to Shakespeare's manuscript, then, is the first Quarto, on which the present edition is based. However, like most editions of Elizabethan plays, the first Quarto was not well printed. A modern editor is obliged to clear up inconsistencies and correct certain errors made in the printing-house. Some are extremely obvious. For example, at II.2.49 the first Quarto has *Nay god Lysander*. This is corrected in the second Quarto and the Folio to *Nay good Lysander*. Occasionally the Folio happily provides a solution for a serious misprint in the first Quarto. For example, at V.1.188 the Quarto reads, nonsensically, *Thy stones with lime and hair knit now againe*. This is corrected in the Folio to *knit vp in thee*. Other difficulties are less easily solved. There are times when the Quartos and the Folio make good but different sense, and the editor has to decide whether he thinks the Folio's reading may reasonably be considered to be a correction of, or Shakespeare's own improvement on, that of the Quartos. An example is at V.1.122 where the Quartos have *he hath plaid on this Prologue* and the Folio *hee hath plaid on his Prologue*. There is very little to choose between these two readings. There are also some difficulties which cannot be certainly solved. Examples are mentioned in the Commentary to III.1.75–7 and V.1.203.

The alterations made in the Folio which affect the staging of the play are slight but interesting. Obviously they reflect stage practice in Shakespeare's lifetime, or shortly after. One can see a real advantage to the actors in having V.1.44–60 broken up between Lysander and Theseus as in the Folio, instead of being spoken by Theseus alone, as indicated in the Quartos. We cannot tell whether such alterations were made by Shakespeare, or with his approval. The division into acts is first made in the Folio. It is worth remembering that in writing the play Shakespeare does not seem to have had these act divisions in mind.

A Midsummer Night's Dream is sometimes thought to have undergone revision after its first performance. This theory is connected with the belief that it was written for a special occasion. There is no certain evidence to support it. However, Professor John Dover Wilson, in the New Cambridge edition, brilliantly demonstrated that Shakespeare made additions to the play at the beginning of Act V. Dover Wilson believed that the interval between the original composition and the rewriting was 'a matter of years rather than of hours or days', but this judgement is based only on considerations of style and is not universally accepted. The additions may well have been made during the process of composition. The demonstration depends on the fact that in the first Quarto some of the verse is printed irregularly. The following well-known passage (V.1.4–22) is printed here as it appears in the Quarto except that the disarranged verse is printed in italic type, and strokes indicate the true ends of the verse lines:

Louers, and mad men haue such seething braines,
Such shaping phantasies, that apprehend | more,
Then coole reason euer comprehends. | The lunatick,
The louer, and the Poet | are of imagination all compact. |
One sees more diuels, then vast hell can holde:
That is the mad man. The louer, all as frantick,

Sees Helens beauty in a brow of Ægypt.
The Poets eye, in a fine frenzy, rolling, | *doth glance*
From heauen to earth, from earth to heauen. | *And as*
Imagination bodies forth | *the formes of things*
Vnknowne: the Poets penne | *turnes them to shapes,*
And giues to ayery nothing, | *a locall habitation,*
And a name. | Such trickes hath strong imagination,
That if it would but apprehend some ioy,
It comprehends some bringer of that ioy.
Or in the night, imagining some feare,
How easie is a bush suppos'd a Beare?

The regularly divided lines form a consecutive passage, complete in itself. It appears that the lines in italics were written, perhaps in the margin of the manuscript, in such a way that the compositor was not clear how they should have been divided. Altogether there are twenty-nine lines, all at the beginning of Act V, which seem to have been added.

The following notes record the points in the text of the play at which the present edition departs significantly from the first Quarto. Simple misprints, mislineations, and so on are not recorded. Quotations from the Quartos and the Folio are printed as they appear in those editions, that is, in old spelling and so on, though minor typographical differences from one edition to another are not noted. The more interesting textual points are discussed in the Commentary.

In the Account of the Text and the Commentary the first Quarto (1600) is referred to as Q1, the second Quarto (1619) as Q2, both Quartos as Q and the first Folio (1623) as F.

COLLATIONS

1

The following is a list of readings in the present text of *A Midsummer Night's Dream* which differ from Q1 and were first made in Q2, followed by F. Most of them are corrections of obvious misprints. (Q1's reading is printed on the right of the square bracket.)

I.I

    4 wanes] waues

II.2

    36 Be it] bet it
    49 good] god
    53 is] it

III.I

    50 BOTTOM] *Cet.*

III.2

    299 gentlemen] gentleman
    426 shalt] shat

IV.I

    127 is] *not in* Q1
    205 to expound] expound

V.I

    303 and prove] and yet prooue

2

The following readings in the present text of *A Midsummer Night's
Dream* depart from those of both Quartos and are first found in
the Folio. (The reading of the Quartos is given on the right of
the square bracket.)

II.I

    158 the] *not in* Q
    201 nor] not

III.I

    76 Odours – odours! (Odours, odours, F)] Odours,
      odorous.
    81 PUCK] *Quin.*

III.2

    19 mimic (Mimmick F)] Minnick Q1; Minnock Q2
    220 passionate] *not in* Q

IV.I

    207 a patched] patcht a

IV.2

    3 STARVELING] *Flut.*

V.I

34 our] Or
122 his] this
154 Snout] *Flute*
188 up in thee] now againe
342 BOTTOM] *Lyon*

3

The following readings in the present text of *A Midsummer Night's Dream* differ from those of both Quartos and the Folio. Most of these alterations were first made by eighteenth-century editors. Those that are of special interest are discussed in the Commentary. (The reading on the right of the square bracket is common to Q and F unless otherwise indicated.)

The Characters in the Play] *not in* Q, F
I.1

10 New-bent] Now bent
24, 26 'Stand forth, Demetrius' *and* 'Stand forth, Lysander' *are printed as stage directions in* Q, F
136 low] loue
187 Yours would] Your words
191 I'd (ile Q1; Ile Q2, F)
216 sweet] sweld
219 stranger companies] strange companions
I.2

24–5 To the rest. – Yet] To the rest yet
26–7 split: | The] split the
II.1

79 Aegles] Eagles
101 cheer] heere
109 thin] chinne
190 slay . . . slayeth] stay . . . stayeth
II.2

9 FIRST FAIRY] *not in* Q, F
13, 24 CHORUS] *not marked in* Q, F

III.1

      63 and let] or let

      97 fair, fair Thisbe] faire, *Thysby*

    118 ousel] Woosell

  154–8 PEASEBLOSSOM . . . go] *Fairies. Readie:* and I, and I, and I. Where shall we goe

170–73 PEASEBLOSSOM . . . MUSTARDSEED Hail!] 1. *Fai.* Haile mortall, haile. | 2. *Fai.* Haile. | 3. *Fai.* Haile.

  190 your more] you more

III.2

    80 so] *not in* Q, F

  213 first, like] first life

  250 prayers] praise

257–8 No, no. He'll | Seem to break loose] No, no: heele | Seeme to break loose; Q1; No, no, Sir, seeme to breake loose; F. *The present edition follows C. J. Sisson's interpretation of this passage*

  258 he] you

  406 Speak. In some bush?] Speake in some bush

  451 To] *not in* Q, F

IV.1

    40 all ways] alwaies

    72 o'er] or

    81 sleep of all these five] sleepe: of all these, fine

  116 Seemed] Seeme

  132 rite] right

  171 saw] see

V.1

  191 My love! Thou art my love] My loue thou art, my loue

  204 mural down] Moon vsed Q; morall downe F

  214 beasts in: a] beasts, in a

304–5 How chance Moonshine is gone before Thisbe comes back and finds her lover?] How chance Moone-shine is gone before? *Thisby* comes backe, and findes her louer.

  362 behowls] beholds

409–10 *The second of these lines is printed before the first in* Q, F

4 Stage Directions

The stage directions of the present edition are based on those of
the first Quarto, though with reference to those of the second
Quarto and the Folio. Certain clarifications and regularizations
have been made; for example, at the beginning of Act III, Scene
1, the first Quarto has '*Enter the Clownes*'. The names of the
mechanicals (or 'clowns') have been substituted. Also some directions for stage business required by the dialogue have been added.
The more interesting stage directions of the Quartos and Folio
that have been altered are given below in their original form.
Also listed are the more important editorial additions.

I.1

   0 *Enter Theseus, Hippolyta, Philostrate, and attendants*]
     Enter Theseus, Hippolita, *with others* Q, F
  15 *Exit Philostrate*] *not in* Q, F
  19 *Enter Egeus and his daughter Hermia, and Lysander,*
     and Demetrius] *Enter* Egeus *and his daughter* Hermia,
     and Lysander *and* Helena, *and* Demetrius Q1

III.1

   0 *Enter the clowns: Bottom, Quince, Snout, Starveling,*
     Flute, and Snug] *Enter the Clownes* Q, F

III.2

404, 412 *Lysander's exit and re-entry are not in* Q, F

IV.1

  83 (*to Bottom, removing the ass's head*)] *not in* Q, F
 137 *Horns sound; the lovers wake; shout within; the lovers*
     start up] *Shoute within: they all start vp. Winde hornes*
     Q; *Hornes and they wake* | *Shout within, they all start*
     vp F

V.1

   0 *Enter Theseus, Hippolyta, Philostrate, lords, and atten-*
     dants] *Enter* Theseus, Hippolita, *and* Philostrate Q;
     Enter Theseus, Hippolita, Egeus and his Lords F
 107 *Flourish of trumpets*] *Flor. Trum.* F (*not in* Q)
 125 *Enter Bottom as Pyramus, Flute as Thisbe, Snout as*

Wall, Starveling as Moonshine, and Snug as Lion; a
trumpeter before them] Enter Pyramus, and Thysby, and
Wall, and Moone-shine, and Lyon Q1; Enter Pyramus
and Thisby, Wall, Moone-shine, and Lyon Q2; Tawyer
with a Trumpet before them. Enter Pyramus and Thisby,
Wall, Moone-shine, and Lyon F

150 Exeunt Quince, Bottom, Flute, Snug, and Starveling]
Exit Lyon, Thysby, and Mooneshine Q, F, after line
152; F adds 'Exit all but Wall' after line 150

174 Wall holds up his fingers] not in Q, F

256 Lion roars. Flute as Thisbe runs off] The Lion roares,
Thisby runs off F (not in Q)

260 Lion tears Thisbe's mantle. Exit] not in Q, F

352 A dance. Exeunt Bottom and his fellows] not in Q, F

390 Song and dance] not in Q, F

Commentary

The act and scene divisions are those of Peter Alexander's edition of the *Complete Works* (1951). Biblical references are to the Bishops' Bible (1568, etc.), the official English translation of Elizabeth's reign. For Q, Q1, Q2 and F, see An Account of the Text. In quotations from the Quartos and the Folio the 'long s' (ſ) has been replaced by 's'.

I.I

4 *lingers*: Delays.

6 *withering out*: Causing to dwindle. The idea is that the young man has inherited his father's estate, but has to go on paying some of the income to the widow.

7 *steep themselves*: Be absorbed.

13 *pert*: Lively, brisk.

15 *companion*: Fellow (used contemptuously).
pomp: Procession, pageant, ceremony.

16–17 *Hippolyta, I wooed thee with my sword . . . injuries*: Theseus captured Hippolyta in conquering the Amazons.

19 *triumph*: Public festivity and show of rejoicing.
Egeus: Pronounced Egee-us: three syllables.
Hermia: We learn from III.2.257 and 288 that Hermia is short and dark.

24, 26 *Stand forth, Demetrius* and *Stand forth, Lysander*: Printed as stage directions in the early editions. The fact that they complete the verse lines shows that they should be spoken.

32 *stolen the impression of her fantasy*: Craftily impressed
   yourself on her fancy. Obviously the metre demands
   some elision. The actor is likely to pronounce *stolen*
   as one syllable ('stol'n') and *the impression* as three
   ('th'impression'). There are many other examples in
   the play of unaccented or lightly accented syllables in
   verse lines. Editors frequently mark such syllables with
   an apostrophe. But Shakespeare's verse does not con-
   form to a mathematically exact system of versi-
   fication, and we cannot always be sure whether for
   instance an unaccented syllable at the end of a line
   should be sounded or not (III.2.345: *This is thy negligence. Still thou mistakest*). Also the marking of such
   syllables may suggest an abruptness of speaking which
   is neither necessary nor desirable. For instance, II.1.191
   reads *Thou toldest me they were stolen unto this wood*.
   Obviously the second syllable in *toldest* and *stolen* will
   be very lightly stressed. Yet an actor may find it easier
   to sound the syllables while preserving the rhythm
   rather than try to pronounce something printed as
   'told'st' and 'stol'n'. For these reasons, unaccented
   syllables that may have been elided for metrical reasons
   are generally printed in full in the present edition.

33 *gauds*: Playthings, toys.
   conceits: Fancy things, trinkets.

34 *Knacks*: Knick-knacks.

35 *prevailment*: Power.

39 *Be it so*: If.

45 *Immediately*: Expressly.

54 *in this kind*: In this respect.
   voice: Approval, favour.

56–7 *my eyes . . . his judgement*: The play is to be much
   concerned with troubles caused by a dislocation
   between the evidence of the senses and the reasoning
   power.

60 *concern*: Befit.

65 *die the death*: Be put to death by legal process.

68, 74 *blood*: Passions, feelings.

70 *livery*: Habit, costume.

71 *For aye*: For ever.
    mewed: Confined.
73 *moon*: As Diana, goddess of chastity.
76 *earthlier happy*: Happier on earth.
    rose distilled: Roses were distilled to make perfumes.
80 *patent*: Privilege.
81 *his lordship*: That is, the lordship of him; the metrical
    stress is on *his*.
92 *crazèd title*: Flawed, unsound claim.
98 *estate unto*: Settle, bestow upon.
99–110 *I am, my lord . . . inconstant man*: Shaw writes: 'it
    should be clear to any stage manager that Lysander's
    speech, beginning "I am, my lord, as well derived as
    he", should be spoken privately and not publicly to
    Theseus' (*Saturday Review*, 13 July 1895).
99 *derived*: Descended.
100 *well possessed*: Rich.
101 *My fortunes . . . ranked*: My fortunes (are) of as good
    a rank. (Abbreviation was not always clearly indicated
    by Elizabethan printers, so it may be that we should
    read 'My fortune's'.)
102 *with vantage*: Better.
106 *to his head*: To his face, in his teeth.
110 *spotted*: Stained, polluted.
117 *arm*: Prepare.
120 *extenuate*: Mitigate, relax.
123 *go along*: Come along with me.
124 *business*: Pronounced with three syllables.
125 *Against*: In preparation for.
126 *nearly that concerns*: That closely concerns.
130 *Belike*: Perhaps.
131 *Beteem*: Allow.
134–40 *The course of true love . . . eyes*: Shaw comments:
    'Shakespeare makes the two star-crossed lovers speak
    in alternate lines with an effect which sets the whole
    scene throbbing with their absorption in one another'
    (*Saturday Review*, 13 July 1895).
135 *blood*: Birth, rank.
137 *misgraffèd*: Badly matched.

143 *momentary*: An obsolete form of 'momentary'.

145 *collied*: Blackened, darkened.

146 *spleen*: Impulse; fit of anger or passion.

149 *quick*: This may be taken either as an adjective (alive, vital) or an adverb (quickly).

155 *fancy*: Love.

156 *persuasion*: Principle, doctrine.

158 *revenue*: Pronounced here with the accent on the second syllable.

159–60 *From Athens is her house remote seven leagues;* | *And she respects me as her only son*: Dr Johnson and some later editors reverse the order of these lines. This may be an improvement in fluency, but it brings together two clauses beginning with 'and', which seems clumsy. There is no need for the alteration.

165 *without*: Outside.

167 *To do observance to a morn of May*: To celebrate Mayday. The celebrations, common in Elizabethan times, if not in the classical ones in which the action is ostensibly set, generally took place in the woods outside a town.

170 *his best arrow with the golden head*: Cupid was said to carry arrows of lead to repel love, and arrows of gold to cause it. The legend is given in Ovid's *Metamorphoses* (Book I), well known to Shakespeare, and anyhow was common knowledge.

171 *By the simplicity of Venus' doves*: Hermia moves from blank verse into rhyming couplets for her vow. The remainder of the scene is in couplets.
     simplicity: Innocence, guilelessness.
     Venus' doves: Doves were sacred to Venus, and drew her car. The last stanza of Shakespeare's *Venus and Adonis*, written in around 1593, within a year or two of *A Midsummer Night's Dream*, is:

> Thus weary of the world, away she hies,
> And yokes her silver doves by whose swift aid
> Their mistress, mounted, through the empty skies
> In her light chariot quickly is conveyed,

Holding their course to Paphos, where their queen
Means to immure herself and not be seen.

173–4 *fire which burned the Carthage queen . . . sail was seen*:
Dido, Queen of Carthage, burned herself on a funeral
pyre when her lover, the Trojan Aeneas, sailed away.
The story is told by Virgil in the *Aeneid*, and is the
subject of a play by Marlowe and Nashe dating probably from a few years before *A Midsummer Night's
Dream*.

179 *Helena*: We learn from III.2.187 and 291–3 that Helena
is tall and fair.

182 *fair*: Beauty, kind of beauty. F reads *you fair*, which
makes equally good sense; but Q's reading is more
likely to be Shakespeare's.

183 *lodestars*: Leading or guiding stars.

184 *tuneable*: Tuneful, musical.

186 *favour*: Good looks.

190 *bated*: Excepted.

191 *translated*: Transformed.

207 *That he hath turned a heaven unto a hell*: This notion
is varied at II.1.243–4, when Helena says of Demetrius:

I'll follow thee, and make a heaven of hell,
To die upon the hand I love so well.

209 *Phoebe*: The moon.

212 *still*: Always.

213 *Athens*: The noun is used as an adjective, as in *the
Carthage queen* (173).

214–220 *where often you and I . . . playfellow*: The reference to
the girlhood friendship of Hermia and Helena looks
forward to the scene of their quarrel, to which it is an
ironic background.

219 *stranger companies*: The company of strangers. The
early editions read *strange companions*. A rhyme to *eyes*
is required.

223 *lovers' food*: The sight of each other.

226 *other some*: Some others.

232–3 *Things base and vile . . . form and dignity*: This looks
        forward especially to Titania's infatuation with Bottom.

232 *quantity*: Proportion.

234 *Love looks not with the eyes, but with the mind*: That is,
     love is prompted not by the objective evidence of the
     senses, but by the fancies of the mind.

237 *figure*: Symbolize, represent.

240 *waggish*: Playful.

242 *eyne*: Eyes (an old form, common in Shakespeare,
     especially in rhymed passages).

248 *intelligence*: News, information.

249 *a dear expense*: Perhaps 'an expense of trouble worth
     making', or possibly 'it will cost him dear', that is,
     'merely to thank me will be painful to him'.

I.2

        As is common in Shakespeare and in Elizabethan plays
        generally, the characters of low social standing speak
        in prose. No particular location for this scene is
        suggested. It takes place somewhere in Athens.

    0 *Bottom*: As a weaver's term, a bottom was the object
       on which thread was wound. 'Bottom' as 'posterior' is
       not recorded till late in the eighteenth century, but the
       name 'Mistress Frigbottom' in Thomas Dekker's *The
       Shoemaker's Holiday* (1600) shows that this sense
       existed in Shakespeare's time.
       Starveling: Tailors were proverbially thin.

    2 *generally*: Bottom's mistaken way of saying 'sever-
       ally', that is, individually.

    5 *interlude*: Play.

11–12 *The most lamentable comedy . . .*: The title of the
        mechanicals' play parodies ones such as 'A lamentable
        tragedy mixed full of pleasant mirth, containing the
        life of Cambyses, King of Persia', published about
        1570. See also V.1.56–7, where the play is described as
        *A tedious brief scene of young Pyramus | And his love
        Thisbe; 'very tragical mirth'*.

   15 *Masters, spread yourselves*: It is not clear exactly what
        action is intended here. Some directors have the
        mechanicals seated on a bench.

24 *condole*: Lament, express grief.

25 *humour*: Inclination, fancy.

26 *Ercles*: Hercules. This may allude to a ranting role in
a particular play, now lost.

   part to tear a cat in: The phrase, proverbial now for a
ranting role, may have been so in Shakespeare's time.

27–34 *The raging rocks . . . Fates*: This may be a quotation
from a lost play. More probably it is Shakespeare's
burlesque of the kind of writing found in two somewhat similar passages of John Studley's translation
(1581) of Seneca's *Hercules Oetaeus*:

> O lord of ghosts, whose fiery flash
>   That forth thy hand doth shake
> Doth cause the trembling lodges twain
>   Of Phoebus' car to quake . . .
> The roaring rocks have quaking stirred,
>   And none thereat hath pushed;
> Hell gloomy gates I have brast ope
>   Where grisly ghosts all hushed
> Have stood.

31 *Phibbus' car*: The chariot of Phoebus, the sun god.
Phibbus, Q1's spelling, may represent Bottom's idio-
syncratic pronunciation.

37 *condoling*: Pathetic.

41 *a wandering knight*: A knight-errant (a typical role in
a play).

43 *let not me play a woman*: A reminder that women's parts
were played by boys and young men in Shakespeare's
time.

45 *mask*: A customary item of ladies' costume in Shakespeare's time.

47 *An*: If.

48 *Thisne*: Probably the spelling represents Bottom's
pronunciation. But some commentators believe that
Shakespeare wrote *thisne*, meaning 'in this manner'.
The word is not found elsewhere in Shakespeare's
writings.

56–9 *Thisbe's mother . . . Pyramus' father . . . Thisbe's father*:
These characters do not appear in the play as acted.
There are other discrepancies between the play as
projected and as performed. A realistic explanation
should not be sought.

76 *aggravate*: Bottom means 'moderate'. Mistress Quickly
makes the same error (*Henry IV, Part II*, II.4.157):
'I beseek you now, aggravate your choler.'

77 *roar you*: A colloquialism: 'roar for you', or simply
'roar'.
sucking: Unweaned.

78 *an 'twere*: As if it were.

80 *proper*: Handsome.

83–9 *What beard . . . yellow*: Bottom's interest in the colour
of beards is perhaps appropriate to his craft of weaver.

87 *orange-tawny*: Dark yellow.
purple-in-grain: Dyed with a fast purple or red.

88 *French-crown-colour*: Light yellow like a gold coin. (The
French *écu* seems to be alluded to mainly for the sake
of the joke that follows.)

90 *crowns*: Heads. *French crown* refers to the baldness
produced by venereal disease, particularly associated
by the English with France.

97 *properties*: Stage requisites.

100 *obscenely*: The point lies rather in the unfitness of this
word than in what Bottom intended. He may have
meant 'seemly'. Cf. Costard in *Love's Labour's Lost*,
IV.1.144: 'When it comes so smoothly off, so obscenely
as it were, so fit.'
be perfect: Know your lines.

103 *hold, or cut bowstrings*: This is an expression in archery
of uncertain meaning. It is reasonably interpreted as
'keep your promise or be disgraced'.

II.1

With this scene the play moves into the wood. It is
the night of Lysander's and Hermia's attempt to
escape from Athens, that is, 'tomorrow night' in relation to the first scene. The rhyming verse used for
the opening conversation between Puck and the Fairy

forms an immediate contrast with the mechanicals'
prose.

o *at one door . . . at another*: A common direction in
Elizabethan plays, referring to the doors at the sides
of the stage.

Puck: Puck is often referred to in stage directions
and speech-prefixes of the early editions as Robin
Goodfellow, and is so spoken of and addressed in
the dialogue. A 'puck' is a devil or an imp. Properly
the character in the play is Robin Goodfellow, a
puck.

Robin Goodfellow's appearance is described in a
stage direction of *Grim the Collier of Croydon*, a play
of unknown authorship written about 1600: 'Enter
Robin Goodfellow, in a suit of leather close to his
body; his face and hands coloured russet-colour, with
a flail.'

2 *Over hill, over dale . . .*: The Fairy (commonly played
by a young woman in modern productions, but
presumably by a boy in Shakespeare's time) is given
a new verse form.

4 *pale*: Fenced land, park (that is, the fairies wander over
both public and private land).

7 *moon's sphere*: According to the astronomical notions
of Shakespeare's day, the moon was fixed in a hollow
crystalline sphere or globe which itself revolved round
the earth each twenty-four hours.

9 *orbs*: Fairy rings – circles of darker grass.

10 *pensioners*: Queen Elizabeth was attended by fifty handsome young gentlemen-pensioners, her royal body-
guard, who were splendidly dressed. The word carries
no implications of poverty.

16 *lob*: Clown, lout. (Puck is clearly among the least ethereal of fairies.)

17 *elves*: Fairy boys (that is, presumably, Cobweb,
Peaseblossom, Moth and Mustardseed).

20 *passing*: Exceedingly.
fell: Fierce, angry.

22 *Indian*: Oberon and Titania are again associated with

India at 69 and 124. Titania gives a different account
of the boy (123–37).

23 *changeling*: Usually a child left by fairies in exchange
for one stolen, but here, the stolen child. The word
has three syllables.

25 *trace*: Range, track through.

26 *perforce*: By force.

29 *starlight sheen*: Shining light of the stars.

30 *square*: Quarrel.

32 *making*: Form, shape, build.

33 *shrewd*: Mischievous.

35 *villagery*: Villages.

36 *Skim milk*: Steal cream.
  quern: Hand-mill for grinding corn. Puck is either
  grinding meal himself or mischievously labouring to
  cause the grinding to fail.

37 *bootless*: Fruitlessly. Puck prevents the milk from
turning to butter.

38 *barm*: Froth on ale.

39 *Mislead*: That is, with false fire. Puck later (III.1.103–5)
declares his intention of doing this to the mechanicals.

40 *Hobgoblin*: Another name for Robin Goodfellow.

45 *bean-fed*: Field beans were used as food for horses, and
were also known as horse-beans.
  beguile: Trick.

47 *gossip*: Old woman, crony.

48 *crab*: Crab-apple; an ingredient in a drink.

50 *dewlap*: Skin hanging from the neck; or (possibly) breasts.

51 *aunt*: Old woman, gossip.
  saddest: Most serious.

54 *And 'Tailor' cries*: The exact meaning is unknown. Dr
Johnson (in his notes on the play) writes: 'The custom
of crying "tailor" at a sudden fall backwards I think
I remember to have observed. He that slips beside his
chair falls as a tailor squats upon his board.' *Tailor* may
mean 'posterior'.

55 *choir*: Company.

56 *waxen*: Increase.
  neeze: Sneeze.

57 *wasted*: Spent.

59 *Titania*: In the classical pronunciation (which Shake-
    speare probably followed) the first two vowels would
    be long: that is, the first syllable would be pronounced
    'tight', and the name would rhyme with 'mania'.

60 *Ill met by moonlight, proud Titania*: The entrance of
    Titania and Oberon is marked by a change from
    rhyming to blank verse.

61 *Fairy, skip hence*: This is often emended to 'Fairies';
    but Titania may be addressing the Fairy who has been
    speaking to Oberon's follower, Puck.

64–5 *know | When*: Know of occasions when.

66, 68 *Corin . . . Phillida*: Type-names of the love-sick shep-
    herd and his beloved.

69 *step*: Perhaps 'limit of travel or exploration', resem-
    bling the phrase in *Much Ado About Nothing*
    (II.1.243–5): 'I will fetch you a tooth-picker now from
    the furthest inch of Asia.' 'Steppe', meaning a great
    plain, was probably not a known word at the time. Q2
    and F read *steepe* which may be correct, referring to a
    mountain, perhaps of the Himalayas.

70 *Amazon*: That is, Hippolyta, Queen of the Amazons.

71 *buskined*: Wearing hunting boots. Hippolyta was
    known as a huntress.

75 *Glance at*: Hit at, reflect upon.

78–80 *Perigenia . . . Aegles . . . Ariadne . . . Antiopa*: All loved
    by Theseus. Shakespeare seems to have taken the names
    from the *Life of Theseus* in his great source-book, Sir
    Thomas North's translation of Plutarch's *Lives of the
    Noble Grecians and Romans* (1579), where the first
    appears as 'Perigouna'.

80 *Ariadne*: The legend of Ariadne's helping Theseus to
    thread the labyrinth in which the Minotaur was
    confined, and his deserting her, was well known.

82 *middle summer's spring*: The beginning (*spring*) of mid-
    summer.

84 *pavèd*: Pebbled.

85 *in*: On.
    margent: Shore.

86 *ringlets*: Dances in the form of a ring (the meaning
    'lock of hair' is not recorded before 1667).

86   *to*: To the sound of.

90   *Contagious*: Pestilential, harmful.

91   *pelting*: Paltry.

92   *continents*: Banks.

97   *murrion flock*: Flock infected with murrion (or 'murrain'), a disease of sheep and cattle.

98   *nine men's morris*: Area marked out in squares for the game of the same name, a sort of open-air draughts, in which each player has nine pieces.

99   *quaint mazes*: Intricate arrangements of paths, normally kept visible by being frequently trodden.
      wanton green: Luxuriant grass.

101 *cheer*: A commonly accepted emendation for 'here' in the early editions, which may however be correct. 'Here' seems weak, whereas *cheer* would look forward to the following line.

103 *Therefore*: This repeats the *Therefore* of 88.

104 *washes*: Moistens, wets.

105 *rheumatic*: Characterized by 'rheum', that is, colds, coughs, etc. (The accent is on the first syllable.)

106 *distemperature*: The word means both 'ill-humour, discomposure' and 'bad weather'.

109 *Hiems*: Winter personified. He is introduced into the closing episode of *Love's Labour's Lost* (V.2.880): 'This side is Hiems, winter; this Ver, the spring'.

112 *childing*: Fertile, fruitful (autumn as the season of harvest).
      change: Exchange.

113 *wonted*: Customary.
      mazèd: Amazed, bewildered.

114 *increase*: (Seasonal) products.

116 *debate*: Quarrel.

123 *votaress*: A woman under vow (in Titania's *order*).

127 *traders*: Trading ships.

140 *round*: Round dance.

142 *spare*: Avoid.

144–5 *Not for thy fairy kingdom! . . . Stay*: As often, a couplet is used to mark the end of an episode.

145 *chide*: Quarrel.

147 *injury*: Insult.

149 *Since*: When.

151 *dulcet*: Sweet.
    breath: Voice, song.

152 *rude*: Rough.

157 *certain*: Sure.

158 *vestal*: Virgin (usually assumed to refer to Queen
    Elizabeth).
    by: In.

159 *loveshaft*: The golden arrow (cf. I.1.170).

163 *And the imperial votaress passed on*: The scansion of
    this line is uncertain. The most satisfactory alterna-
    tives seem to be 'Ánd the impérial vót'ress pássèd ón'
    and 'Ánd the impérial vótaréss páss'd ón'.
    imperial: Majestic, imperious, queenly.

165 *bolt*: Arrow.

168 *love in idleness*: Pansy or heart's ease. The idea that it
    changed from white to purple may have been suggested
    by Ovid's statement in the Pyramus and Thisbe story
    that the mulberry, once 'white as snow', was turned to
    'a deep dark purple colour' by Pyramus's blood.

171 *or . . . or*: Either . . . or.

174 *leviathan*: Sea-monster; to the Elizabethans, a whale.

176–87 *Having once this juice . . . conference*: Oberon addresses
    the audience.

192 *and wood*: And mad.

195 *adamant*: Very hard stone supposed to have magnetic
    properties.

196–7 *But yet you draw not iron . . . true as steel*: Iron is the
    obvious substance to be attracted by adamant; Helena
    stresses her more-than-ordinary fidelity to Demetrius.
    The conceit is somewhat strained, perhaps with a delib-
    erate effect of slightly comic inanity.

199 *speak you fair*: Speak kindly to you.

214 *impeach*: Call in question, discredit.

215 *To leave*: By leaving.

220 *Your virtue is my privilege*: A difficult expression. *virtue*
    probably means 'qualities', 'attractions'. We may para-
    phrase: 'the effect of your qualities upon me puts me

in a privileged position' – that is, because when Demetrius is there the night seems like day.

220 *For that*: Because.

224 *in my respect*: To my mind.

231 *Apollo flies, and Daphne holds the chase*: Daphne, flying from Apollo, was changed into a laurel tree so as to escape him. The story was familiar from Ovid's *Metamorphoses* (Book I).

232 *griffin*: Fabulous monster with the body of a lion but the head, wings, and forehead of an eagle.
    hind: Doe.

233 *bootless*: Useless.

235 *stay*: Wait for.

240 *Your wrongs do set a scandal on my sex*: The wrongs that you do me cause me to act in a manner that disgraces my sex.

241 *We cannot fight for love . . .*: The scene moves into couplets, partly perhaps in preparation for Oberon's lyrical lines from 249.

244 *upon*: By.

245 *Fare thee well, nymph*: Oberon, who has been an 'invisible' spectator, now comes forward.

250 *oxlips*: Flowering herbs, hybrids between the cowslip and the primrose.
    grows: The singular verb with a plural subject was not unusual in Elizabethan English.

251 *woodbine*: Honeysuckle.

252 *muskroses . . . eglantine*: Wild roses . . . sweet-briar.

253 *some time*: For some part of.

255 *throws*: Throws off, casts.

256 *Weed*: Garment.

266 *fond on*: In love, infatuated with.

267 *ere the first cock crow*: Some supernatural beings were thought to be unable to bear daylight. At III.2.386 Oberon is dissociated from the ghosts and spirits who *wilfully themselves exile from light*. This seems a way of stressing his generally benevolent function.

II.2

This scene follows immediately on the preceding one. The place is the bank mentioned by Oberon at II.1.249.

1 *roundel*: Round dance, all joining hands.

2 *third part of a minute*: Suggesting great rapidity of action on the part of the fairies.

4 *reremice*: Bats.

7 *quaint*: Pretty, dainty.

9 *double*: Forked.

11 *Newts and blindworms*: Though neither is in fact harmful, they were thought to be so in Shakespeare's time. The witches' cauldron in *Macbeth* includes 'Eye of newt' and 'blind-worm's sting' (IV.1.14, 16).

13 *Philomel*: The classical name for the nightingale.

20 *spiders*: Also thought to be poisonous.

21 *longlegged spinners*: Probably daddy-long-legs.

30 *Titania sleeps*: There is no break in the action between Titania's falling asleep and her awakening by Bottom at III.1.122. She must apparently remain onstage throughout this time. However, it is not necessary for her to be visible to the audience. It is possible that on the Elizabethan stage she occupied a recess that could be curtained off at the end of Oberon's spell (40), and that the curtain was drawn to reveal her during the first verse of Bottom's song (III.1.118).

32 *One aloof stand sentinel*: Perhaps on an Elizabethan stage one fairy would have been stationed on the upper stage (*aloof*). Oberon, whether or not his 'invisibility' was effective with his fellow-fairies, would have been able to outwit the sentinel by confining his movements to the area at the back of the stage where, presumably, Titania sleeps. In stage practice, the sentinel is sometimes kidnapped by Oberon's attendants.

33–40 *What thou seest . . . near*: Oberon's spell is distinguished by the use of trochaic, rhyming verse. This tripping measure is used elsewhere by fairy characters, e.g. the Fairy, II.1.6–13; Puck, II.2.72–89; Oberon for other spells at III.2.102–9 and IV.1.70–73, and Puck and Oberon in their following dialogue; Puck at

III.2.396–9, 437–41; Puck, Oberon and Titania at
IV.1.92–101, and in the closing speeches, V.1.361–428.

36 *ounce*: Lynx.

37 *Pard*: Leopard.

48 *troth*: An old spelling of 'truth', preserved for the rhyme.

51 *take the sense*: Take the true meaning.

52 *Love . . . conference*: In lovers' conversation (*conference*)
their love enables them truly to understand each other.

58 *lie*: A pun on the senses 'lie down' and 'deceive'.

70 *Here is my bed*: That is, at some distance from Hermia.

74 *approve*: Test.

76 *Who is here*: Puck mistakes Lysander for Demetrius.

78 *he my master said*: He that my master said.

85 *owe*: Own.

92 *darkling*: In darkness (the reminder was especially
necessary in the open-air Elizabethan theatre).

94 *fond*: Foolish.

95 *grace*: Answer to prayer.

105 *sphery eyne*: Star-like eyes.

110 *Transparent*: Means both 'lacking in deceit; able to be
seen through' and 'bright'.
art: Magic power.

120 *raven*: Cf. III.2.257, where Lysander calls Hermia
Ethiope. She is presumably dark in hair or complexion.

121 *The will of man is . . . swayed*: Lysander ironically
attributes to his reason the change in his affections that
has been brought about by Puck.

121 *will*: Desire.

124 *ripe not*: *ripe* is a verb.

125 *And touching now the point of human skill*: And I now
reaching the highest point of human capacity.

127–8 *your eyes, where I o'erlook . . . book*: Shakespeare
expresses a similar idea in *Love's Labour's Lost*
(IV.3.326–9):

> From women's eyes this doctrine I derive:
> They sparkle still the right Promethean fire;
> They are the books, the arts, the academes,
> That show, contain, and nourish all the world.

127 *o'erlook*: Look over, read.

138 *gentleness*: Nobility, breeding.

139, 140 *of*: By.

145–6 *as the heresies that men do leave . . . deceive*: As the heresies that men reject are hated most by the very men who had been deceived by them.

149 *address*: Direct, apply.

156 *prey*: Preying.

159 *an if*: If.

160 *of all loves*: For love's sake.

III.1

There is no break between the preceding scene and this one.

0 *clowns*: Rustics.

2 *Pat*: On the dot.

4 *tiring-house*: The dressing-room of the Elizabethan theatre, directly behind the stage. On the Elizabethan stage Bottom would have indicated the *green plot* by pointing to the stage, and the *hawthorn brake* by pointing to the tiring-house.

12 *By'r lakin*: By Our Lady (a light oath).
parlous: Perilous, terrible.

16 *Write me*: Write (a colloquialism).

22 *eight and six*: Lines of eight and six syllables (a metre common in ballads).

27 *yourself*: F has *yourselves* but Q1's singular form may well be a deliberate touch.

39 *it were pity of*: It would be a bad thing for.

46 SNUG: In the early editions the speech-prefix is abbreviated to *Sn*. The line may be spoken by either Snug or Snout.

48 *find out moonshine*: F has the stage direction *Enter Puck* here. This conflicts with the entry given for him in F and Q1 at 69. But it is possible that F's apparently superfluous direction represents an early stage practice of bringing Puck in to watch the mechanicals before he speaks.

51 *Great Chamber*: State room.

53–4 *bush of thorns*: A traditional attribute of the man in the

moon, sometimes said to be the man who picked up a
bundle of sticks on the Sabbath day (Numbers 15:32–6).
There are other explanations. The following passage
from Ben Jonson's masque *News from the New World*
(1620), in reply to a report that a traveller from the
moon has arrived on earth, is an appropriate comment:

FACTOR Where? Which is he? I must see his dog at
    his girdle, and the bush of thorns at his back, ere I
    believe it.
HERALD These are stale ensigns of the stage's man in
    the moon.

54 *disfigure*: Figure.
71 *So near the cradle of the Fairy Queen*: A reminder of
    Titania's presence.
72 *toward*: In preparation.
75–7 *flowers . . . sweet*: This passage is textually difficult. Q
    reads *Odours, odorous* at 76. F reads *Odours, odours*.
    The F reading, adopted here, may be interpreted to
    mean that Bottom ought to say 'the flowers of odours
    savours sweet' (taking *savours* to mean 'savour'; the
    singular agreement with a plural subject would have
    been possible in Elizabethan English). Another
    possible explanation is that *of* is a colloquialism for
    'have'. If this were so, I should read *Odorous, odorous*
    for Quince's correction of Bottom's *odious*. This
    would have the advantage of fitting in better with *hath*
    in *So hath thy breath*.
81 *A stranger Pyramus than e'er played here*: Puck conceives
    the trick that he will play on Bottom.
88 *brisky juvenal*: Brisk youth (the diction is affected).
    eke: Also (an old-fashioned word in Shakespeare's time).
    Jew: Sometimes explained as an abbreviation of 'jewel'
    or 'juvenal', but perhaps no more than a deliberately
    inconsequential piece of padding.
90 *Ninny's tomb*: A *Ninny* is a 'fool'. In Ovid's version of
    the story of Pyramus and Thisbe, they met at the tomb
    of Ninus, mythical founder of Nineveh.

93 *part*: The script given to the actor, containing his speeches and cues.

103 *headless bear*: Headless figures, whether human or animal, were traditional apparitions.

   fire: Will o'the wisp.

105 *at every turn*: F has the stage direction *Enter Piramus with the Asse head*. This seems to be a mistake; but it may be that Bottom goes out at the same time as the other mechanicals, and re-enters at this point.

112–13 *translated*: Transformed. This was a regular meaning; no joke is intended.

118–29 *The ousel cock . . . never so*: Titania had been lulled to sleep with a song of the nightingale (Philomel). She is aroused by Bottom's song of more homely birds.

118 *ousel*: Blackbird.

120 *throstle*: Thrush.

121 *little quill*: Small voice.

122 *What angel wakes me from my flowery bed*: If Titania has been curtained off during her sleep, she must reappear, probably during the first verse of Bottom's song.

124 *plainsong*: Having an unadorned song (normally a noun; here used adjectivally). The allusion is to the cuckoo's repeated call, with its traditional associations of cuckoldry.

127 *set his wit to*: Use his intelligence to answer.

133 *thy fair virtue's force*: The power of your excellent qualities.

139 *gleek*: Make a satirical joke.

146 *still*: Continually, always.

   doth tend upon: That is, waits upon.

149 *jewels from the deep*: There was a belief that precious stones were produced on the seabed.

153 *Moth*: This is a normal Elizabethan spelling of 'mote', which may be what Shakespeare intended. But the association with 'Cobweb' may support the traditional spelling with the modern meaning.

159–69 *Be kind and courteous . . . courtesies*: The repeated rhymes add to the lyrical effect of this speech.

161 *apricocks*: An old form of 'apricots', closer to the word
    from which it is derived.
    dewberries: A kind of blackberry.

165 *light them at the fiery glow-worms' eyes*: Dr Johnson
    tartly comments: 'I know not how Shakespeare, who
    commonly derived his knowledge of nature from his
    own observation, happened to place the glow-worm's
    light in his eyes, which is only in his tail.' (It is not
    certain whether Shakespeare intended *glow-worm's* or
    glow-worms'.)

174 *cry . . . mercy*: Beg pardon (for asking you your names).

178 *cut my finger*: Cobwebs were used to stop bleeding.

181–2 *Squash*: An unripe pea-pod. *Peascod* is a ripe pea-pod.
    Cf. *Twelfth Night*, I.5.151–2: 'Not yet old enough for
    a man, nor young enough for a boy; as a squash is
    before 'tis a peascod.'

187–90 *That same cowardly, giantlike Oxbeef . . . ere now*: Mus-
    tard, of course, is often eaten with beef. Bottom admires
    the patience of Mustardseed's kin in suffering this. By
    made my eyes water he may mean both 'I have wept in
    sympathy with them' and 'they have made my eyes
    smart'.

193–4 *The moon methinks looks with a watery eye . . . flower*:
    There was a belief that dew originated in the moon.

195 *enforcèd*: Violated. (The moon is Diana, the chaste
    goddess.)

196 *Tie up my lover's tongue*: This suggests that Bottom
    may (as he often does in performance) be making invol-
    untary asinine noises.

III.2

Again there is no significant break between the scenes,
in either time or place. However, this scene begins
with a recapitulatory passage between Puck and
Oberon. The end of III.1 would be an appropriate
place for an interval in performance.

0 Q reads *Enter King of Fairies, and Robin Goodfellow*.
    F reads *Enter King of Pharies solus* at the beginning
    of the scene, and *Enter Puck* after 3. F is probably
    closer to stage practice.

5 *night-rule*: Actions (or possibly 'revels', amusements)
of the night.

7 *close*: Private, secret.

9 *patches*: Fools, clowns.
rude mechanicals: Rough working men.

13 *barren sort*: Stupid group.

15 *scene*: Stage.

17 *nole*: Noddle, head.

19 *mimic*: Burlesque actor.

21 *russet-pated choughs*: The chough is a jackdaw. Its head
is grey; but *russet* could mean 'grey' as well as 'reddish'.
many in sort: In a great body, in a flock.

25 *our stamp*: Some editors, following Dr Johnson, emend
to 'a stump'. Fairies, it is argued, do not stamp; and
since Puck is alone, there is no reason why he should
use the plural *our*. But Puck is the most robust of the
fairies; and *our* might well be jocular.

26 *He 'Murder!' cries*: One of them makes an outcry.

30 *From yielders all things catch*: Everything preys on the
timid.

36 *latched*: 'Moistened' (a rare sense) or 'fastened'.

40 *That*: So that.

48 *o'er shoes*: So far gone.

53–5 *This whole earth . . . Antipodes*: *whole* means 'solid';
centre, 'the centre of the earth'. The moon's brother
is the sun. *the Antipodes* means 'those who live on the
other side of the earth'. Hermia's notion is that the
moon, creeping through the earth, will displease (by
bringing night with it) the noontide that the sun is
experiencing among those who live on the other side
of the world. The conceit is strained, no doubt for
comic effect; but it has its place among the play's other
images of cosmic disorder, such as those in Titania's
speech, II.1.81–117.

57 *dead*: Deadly.

61 *sphere*: Orbit.

70–73 *And hast thou killed him sleeping? . . . stung*: This recalls
Hermia's dream that she herself was attacked by a
serpent (II.2.151–6).

70 *brave touch*: Fine stroke! (ironical).

71 *worm*: Serpent.

72 *doubler*: Alluding to the adder's forked tongue, but also including the meaning 'more deceitful'.

74 *spend*: 'Give vent to' or 'waste'.

   misprised mood: *mood* could mean 'anger'. *misprised* means 'misunderstood'. The phrase probably means 'anger based on a misunderstanding'.

78 *An if*: Even if.

   therefore: For that.

81 *whether*: This word seems often to have been spoken as one syllable – 'whe'er'.

84 *heaviness . . . heavier*: Playing on *heavy* as 'sad, heavy-spirited' and 'drowsy'.

85 *For debt that bankrupt sleep doth sorrow owe*: That is, as a result of the sleeplessness caused by sorrow.

87 *tender*: Offer.

   make some stay: Wait awhile.

90 *misprision*: Misunderstanding, mistake.

92–3 *Then fate o'errules . . . oath on oath*: Perhaps, 'If so, fate has taken a hand, since for one man who is true in love there are a million who fail, breaking oath after oath.'

95 *look*: Be sure to.

96 *fancy-sick*: Love-sick.

   cheer: Face, look.

97 *sighs of love, that costs the fresh blood dear*: It was believed that a sigh caused the loss of a drop of blood.

99 *against*: Ready for when.

101 *Tartar*: The Oriental bow was of special power. The image may have come to Shakespeare by way of Golding's translation of Ovid's *Metamorphoses*, X.686–7, 'she | Did fly as swift as arrow from a Turkey bow'.

104 *apple*: Pupil.

113 *fee*: 'Payment' or 'perquisite'.

114 *fond pageant*: Foolish spectacle.

119 *alone*: Probably means 'unique', 'unequalled' rather than 'in itself'.

124 *Look when*: Whenever (a common Elizabethan use).

124–5 *and vows so born . . . all truth appears*: Vows being born so (that is, in tears) are certain to be true.

127 *badge of faith*: That is, tears.

129 *When truth kills truth*: The *truth* that Lysander now tells Helena destroys the *truth* that he formerly told Hermia. The truths conflict to cause a fray that is *holy* because between truths, but *devilish* because the truths are incompatible.

131 *nothing weigh*: Arrive at no weight (because the scales will be equally balanced).

136 *loves not you*: The interruption of the rhyme scheme is appropriate to the sudden change in situation.

141 *Taurus*: A range of mountains in Turkey.

144 *princess*: Paragon.
    seal: Pledge.

152 *gentle*: Perhaps 'noble' rather than (or as well as) 'kind' or 'mild'.

153 *parts*: Qualities.

157 *trim*: Fine (ironical).

159 *sort*: 'Quality' or 'rank'.

160 *extort*: Torture.

169 *I will none*: I want nothing to do with her.

175 *aby*: Pay the penalty for, atone for.

177 *his*: Its.

188 *oes and eyes*: Stars (punningly). An 'o' seems to have been a silver spangle.

194 *in spite of me*: To spite me.

197 *bait*: Torment.

203 *artificial*: Artistically skilful (and, like gods, 'creating').

204 *needles*: *needle* was often pronounced as a monosyllable – 'neele'.

206 *both in one key*: That two singers of one song should be in the same musical key is so obviously desirable that this phrase sometimes causes laughter. But the phrase *voices and minds* in the following line shows that for Shakespeare the *song* and the *key* were distinct and that *in one key* means 'in mental accord'.

208 *incorporate*: Of one body.

213 *Two of the first*: That is, bodies. *first* is a heraldic term, referring back to the divisions of a shield which have already been described. In the shield that Helena is imagining, the same quartering appears more than once, but the whole is *crownèd with one crest* because it belongs to one person.

215 *rent*: Rend, tear.

225 *spurn me with his foot*: Helena had invited Demetrius to spurn her (II.1.205).

237 *Persever*: A form of 'persevere', which in Shakespeare always has the stress on the second syllable.

239 *hold the sweet jest up*: Keep up the joke.

242 *argument*: Subject of joking.

244 *Which death or absence soon shall remedy*: The exaggerated threat helps to preserve the comic tone.

247 *Sweet, do not scorn her so*: Hermia still does not realize that Lysander is in earnest.

255 *withdraw, and prove it too*: That is, 'let us go and decide the matter by duelling'.

257 *Ethiope*: Used insultingly – Hermia is evidently of dark complexion; cf. 263.

257–8 *No, no ... follow*: This passage is textually corrupt. The present reading assumes that Demetrius scornfully says that Lysander will seem to break from Hermia's protectively restraining clutches as if to follow Demetrius to fight with him, but in fact will not turn up.

258 *take on as*: Make a fuss as if (or 'act as if').

263 *tawny Tartar*: Another exaggerated reference to Hermia's dark colouring.

264 *medicine*: Any sort of drug, including poison.
      potion: Also could be used of poison; Q2 and F read *poison*.

267, 268 *bond*: Both 'pledge' and 'tie' (here, Hermia, who is holding Lysander).

282 *canker-blossom*: Worm that cankers the blossom (of love); or, perhaps, 'wild-rose'.

284 *Fine, i'faith*: Helena still thinks that Hermia is joining in the men's derision of her.

300 *curst*: Shrewish, quarrelsome.

310 *stealth*: Stealing away, secret journey.

314 *so*: Provided that.

323 *keen*: Bitter, severe.

 shrewd: Shrewish.

329 *minimus*: Tiny creature.

 knot-grass: A common, low-creeping weed. The juice of it was said to stunt growth.

335 *aby*: Pay for.

339 *coil*: Trouble, bother.

 'long of: Caused by, on account of.

345 *This is thy negligence . . .*: The change into blank verse marks the change in speakers and tone, but the rhymed verse resumes at 350.

 Still: Always, continually.

350 *so far*: At least to this extent.

352 *sort*: Fall out.

353 *As*: In that.

354–95 *Thou seest these lovers . . . ere day*: This conversation between Oberon and Puck is a turning point in the action of the play.

355 *Hie*: Go.

356 *welkin*: Sky.

357 *Acheron*: A river of hell, traditionally black. In *Macbeth* (III.5.15) Shakespeare refers to 'the pit of Acheron'.

359 *As*: That.

361 *wrong*: Insult.

365 *batty*: Bat-like.

367 *virtuous*: Potent.

368 *his*: Its.

370–71 *all this derision . . . vision*: In the epilogue Puck suggests that the play may have the same effect on its audience.

373 *date*: Term, duration.

376 *charmèd*: Bewitched.

380 *Aurora's harbinger*: The herald of the dawn; the morning star.

382 *Damnèd spirits*: The ghosts of the damned.

383 *in crossways and floods have burial*: Suicides were buried at crossroads. *floods* may refer to those who have killed themselves by drowning, or to those who were accidentally drowned and whose souls, according to

ancient belief, could not rest because no burial rites
had been performed.

389 *I with the morning's love have oft made sport*: Some
believe Oberon to say that he has often hunted with
Cephalus, Aurora's (the dawn's) lover. More probably
he is claiming that he has often dallied with Aurora
herself. He is pointing out that he can stay up later
than the other sort of spirits.

399 *Goblin*: Hobgoblin (that is, Puck himself).

400 *Here comes one*: In modern performances artificial
smoke is sometimes used to suggest the fog that Oberon
has instructed Puck to cause (355–7). But the scene can
be equally effective if this is left to the audience's
imagination.

402 *drawn*: With drawn sword.

404 *plainer*: Smoother, more level.

417 *That*: With the result that.

421 *Ho, ho, ho*: This was Puck's traditional cry.

422 *Abide*: Wait for.
    wot: Know.

426 *buy this dear*: Pay dearly for this.

439 *curst*: Cross.

461 *Jack shall have Jill*: A proverb, meaning 'the man shall
have his girl'.

463 *The man shall have his mare again*: Another proverb,
meaning 'all will be well'.

IV.1

At the end of the previous scene F has the stage direction *They sleepe all the Act*. This seems to imply that
in performance there was some sort of a break during
which the lovers remained on stage. It is unlikely that
Shakespeare intended any break here. The lovers sleep
onstage during the scene between Bottom and the
fairies, unremarked by them.

    In this scene Shakespeare mingles verse for Titania
and prose for Bottom.

1 *flowery bed*: It is possible that this would have been
represented by a piece of stage furniture on Shakespeare's stage.

2 *coy*: Caress.

19 *neaf*: Fist.

20 *leave your courtesy*: Either 'stop bowing' or 'put on your hat' (if the fairies wear hats).

22 *Cavalery*: Cavalier (perhaps in imitation of the Italian form, *cavaliere*).

23 *Cobweb*: In fact it is Peaseblossom who has been told to scratch (7). Presumably this is a mistake of Shakespeare's. The alliteration seems intentional.

29 *tongs and the bones*: These were elementary musical instruments. The tongs were struck by a piece of metal. The bones were two flat pieces of bone held between the fingers and rattled against each other, as by Negro minstrels.

Here F has a stage direction *Musicke Tongs, Rurall Musicke*. Music is not demanded by the line, but there may have been some sort of musical comic business at this point. Granville-Barker comments: 'The run of the text here almost forbids any such interruption. The only likely occasion for it is when Peaseblossom and company have been dismissed. There would be a pleasing, fantastic irony in little Titania and her monster being lulled to sleep by the distant sound of the tongs and the bones; it would make a properly dramatic contrast to the "still music" for which she calls a moment later, her hand in Oberon's again. A producer might, without offence, venture on the effect. (But Oberon, by the way, had better stop the noise with a disgusted gesture before he begins to speak.)'

32 *bottle*: Small bundle.

35 *thee new nuts*: Some editors make an addition (for example, 'thee thence . . .') to improve the metre. But as it stands the line gives most effective stress to *new nuts*, as a special treat.

36 *pease*: In Shakespeare's time this was both the singular and the plural form. It both means and sounds the same as 'peas'.

38 *exposition*: He means 'disposition', that is, inclination.

40 *all ways*: In all directions.

41–2 *So doth the woodbine the sweet honeysuckle | Gently*
    entwist: This has caused difficulty. *woodbine* can mean
    'honeysuckle' (II.1.251, and *Much Ado About Nothing*,
    III.1.30). Here it seems to mean 'bindweed', or
    'convolvulus'. 'The honeysuckle . . . always twines in
    a left-handed helix. The bindweed family . . . always
    twines in a right-handed helix. . . . The mixed-up
    violent left–right embrace of the bindweed and honey-
    suckle . . . has long fascinated English poets' (Martin
    Gardner, *The Ambidextrous Universe*, 1964; 1970 edn,
    p. 62).

48 *favours*: Flowers as love-tokens.

53 *orient*: Lustrous.

65 *other*: Others (a common Elizabethanism).

66 *May all*: All may.

68 *fierce*: Wild, extravagant.

72 *Dian's bud*: The herb of II.1.184 and III.2.366. There
    was a herb associated with Diana, the goddess of
    chastity, and supposed to have the power of preserving
    chastity, called *agnus castus*.
    Cupid's flower: The *little western flower* of II.1.166 and
    the stage direction at II.2.32.

79 *Silence awhile*: Presumably Oberon is simply urging his
    companions not to disturb the sleeping lovers and Bottom.

81 *these five*: The lovers and Bottom.

82 *charmeth*: Produces as by a charm.

85 *They dance*: The dance is not merely an added enter-
    tainment. Giving symbolical expression of the reunion
    of the Fairy King and Queen, it marks a turning point
    in the play's action.

89 *prosperity*: Q2 and F, followed by some editors, read
    posterity. At II.1.73 we have *To give their bed joy and*
    prosperity.

94 *sad*: Sober, grave.

96–7 *We the globe can compass soon, | Swifter than the*
    wandering moon: Cf. Puck's claim to *put a girdle round*
    about the earth | In forty minutes (II.1.175–6).

101 *Horns*: The horn was a signalling instrument, not used
    for music.

103 *observation*: An *observance to a morn of May* such as
     that mentioned at I.1.167.
104 *since we have the vaward of the day*: Since it is still early.
     vaward means 'forepart', 'vanguard'.
106 *Uncouple*: Release the dogs (chained together in couples).
111–13 *I was with Hercules and Cadmus once . . . Sparta*: There
     seems to be no basis in legends for this statement, which
     presumably is local colouring.
112–13 *Crete . . . Sparta*: The hounds of both countries were
     famous, as Shakespeare could have known from
     Golding's translation of Ovid's *Metamorphoses*
     (III.247): 'This latter was a hound of Crete, the other
     was of Spart.'
112 *bayed*: Brought to bay.
114 *chiding*: Barking.
117 *musical . . . discord . . . sweet thunder*: Theseus' accept-
     ance of the yoking of opposites here anticipates V.1.60:
     How shall we find the concord of this discord?
119 *flewed*: Having flews, that is, the large chaps of a deep-
     mouthed hound.
     sanded: Of sandy colour.
122–3 *matched in mouth like bells, | Each under each*: The
     notion is illustrated by a passage from Gervase
     Markham's *Country Contentments* (1615):

     If you would have your kennel for sweetness of cry, then
     you must compound it of some large dogs, that have deep,
     solemn mouths and are swift in spending, which must (as it
     were) bear the bass in the consort; then a double number of
     roaring and loud ringing mouths, which must bear the
     counter-tenor; then some hollow, plain, sweet mouths, which
     must bear the mean or middle part; and so with these three
     parts of music you shall make your cry perfect.

     It is unlikely that any pack reached Markham's ideal.
123 *cry*: Pack of hounds.
126 *soft*: 'Stop' rather than 'hush'.
134–5 *is not this the day . . . choice*: Theseus had given Hermia
     till *the next new moon* to make up her mind. See I.1.83–90.

138–9 *Saint Valentine is past!* . . . *now*: It was said that birds
chose their mates on St Valentine's Day (14 February).

140 *Pardon, my lord*: Presumably the lovers kneel, pro-
voking Theseus's *I pray you all, stand up*.

143 *jealousy*: Suspicion.

162 *in fancy*: Impelled by love.

166 *idle gaud*: Worthless toy, trinket. Egeus had accused
Lysander of using gauds to attract Hermia (I.1.33).

172 *like a sickness*: Probably means 'as in sickness'.

188 *with parted eye*: That is, with the eyes out of focus.

190 *like a jewel*: That is, like a precious thing found, and
thus of uncertain ownership.

191–2 *Are you sure | That we are awake*: This sentence is
omitted from F. It is metrically rather awkward, and
its omission may have been deliberate – whether on
Shakespeare's or someone else's part, we cannot tell.

198 *let's*: Q2 and F read *let us*: This regularizes the metre,
and may be correct.

199 *When my cue comes* . . .: Bottom, too, is momentarily
lost between illusion and reality. As he awakes his
mind goes back to the moment of his translation
(III.1.95).

200 *Heigh ho*: A yawn, perhaps with a hint of 'Hee-Haw!'

203 *vision*: The word has been used by Oberon (III.2.371)
and Titania (IV.1.75), and will be repeated by Puck
(V.1.416).

205 *go about*: Try.

207–8 *patched fool*: A fool or jester wearing a patchwork
costume.

208–11 *The eye of man hath not heard, the ear of man hath not
seen, man's hand is not able to taste, his tongue to conceive,
nor his heart to report what my dream was*: The confusion of the functions of senses is used elsewhere in the
play for comic effect (for example, V.1.189–90).
Attention has been drawn to the resemblance to 1
Corinthians 2:9: 'The eye hath not seen, and the ear
hath not heard, neither have entered into the heart of
man, the things which God hath prepared for them
that love him.'

213 *hath no bottom*: Is unfathomable; has no reality.

214 *a play*: Sometimes emended to 'our play' or 'the play';
       a is the reading of the early editions.

216 *her death*: Presumably Thisbe's.

IV.2

With this scene we return to Athens.

4 *transported*: 'Carried off by the fairies' or (euphemisti-
       cally) 'killed'.

5–6 *It goes not forward*: We're not going on with it. F reads
       It goes not forward, doth it? It is just possible that Q's
       division into two sentences represents a deliberate
       pointing of the words.

8 *discharge*: Perform.

9 *wit*: Intellect.

11 *person*: Figure, appearance.

14 *thing of naught*: Something evil.

17 *we had all been made men*: Our fortunes would have
       been made.

18–19 *sixpence a day*: This would have been a princely reward.

20 *An*: If.

24 *courageous*: Perhaps 'encouraging'; or perhaps Quince's
       blunder for 'auspicious'.

33 *presently*: Immediately; very soon.

34 *preferred*: Recommended, put forward.

35 *In any case*: Whatever happens.

V.1

This scene (which forms the complete act) follows in
the evening of the same day. Theseus, Hippolyta, and
the two pairs of young lovers have been married, and
come to a celebration.

This act demonstrates Shakespeare's mastery of
varied styles of both prose and verse. The verse in
particular has great range, including the dignified and
imaginative blank verse of the opening dialogue, the
rather more familiar, somewhat humorous blank verse
of Theseus's conversation with Philostrate, the many
different measures parodied in the play-within-the-
play, and the rhyming trochaic verses of the closing
section.

o   In F *Philostrate* here and elsewhere in Act V is changed
    to *Egeus*. Philostrate's only other appearance is at
    I.I.II, where he has nothing to say. F seems to be econ-
    omizing on actors. It seems desirable that the roles
    should be kept distinct.

3   *antique*: Both 'grotesque' and 'old-fashioned'.
    fairy toys: Idle tales about fairies.

5   *fantasies*: Imaginations.
    apprehend: Imagine, conceive.

6   *comprehends*: Understands.

8   *compact*: Composed.

II *Helen*: Of Troy.
    a brow of Egypt: A gypsy's face.

20 *comprehends*: Includes.

25 *More witnesseth than fancy's images*: Gives evidence of
    more than the creations of the imagination.

27 *admirable*: To be wondered at.

32 *masques*: Courtly entertainments, centred on a dance
    but also having some dramatic content.

34 *after-supper*: The dessert, or 'banquet', of fruits and
    sweetmeats taken to round off the evening meal.

39 *abridgement*: This may mean both 'a shortened version
    of a longer work' and 'something which will make the
    time seem shorter'.

42 *brief*: Short account, summary.

44–60 *The Battle with the Centaurs . . . discord*: In F Lysander
    reads the *brief* and Theseus comments. This may well
    represent the practice of Shakespeare's company.

44–7 *The Battle with the Centaurs . . . Hercules*: Theseus
    himself had taken part in a battle with the Centaurs at
    which Hercules also was present. The story is told in
    Book XII of Ovid's *Metamorphoses*.

47 *my kinsman, Hercules*: That Theseus and Hercules
    'were near kinsmen, being cousins removed by the
    mother's side' is mentioned in Plutarch's *Life of
    Theseus*.

48–9 *The riot of the tipsy Bacchanals,* | *Tearing the Thracian
    singer in their rage*: The *Thracian singer* is Orpheus.
    The story of his being torn to pieces by the Thracian

women under the influence of Bacchic rites is told at
the beginning of Book XI of Ovid's *Metamorphoses*.

50 *device*: Show, performance.

52–3 *The thrice three Muses . . . late deceased in beggary*: It
has been suggested that this refers to the death of some
particular man of learning, variously identified. But
there were many complaints in Shakespeare's time of
the neglect of scholarship and the arts, and it is not
likely that Shakespeare refers to anything more
specifically topical than this literary theme.

55 *sorting with*: Befitting.

59 *strange*: Many editors have felt that emendation is
necessary and have provided an adjective bearing to
snow the relationship of *hot* to *ice*. The passage seems
perfectly satisfactory as it stands.

70 *passion*: The word could be used generally of any
strong feeling, for example, 'idle merriment, | A
passion hateful to my purposes' (*King John*, III.3.46–7).
Its associations with grief as well make it appropriate
in this context of antithesis.

74 *unbreathed*: Unexercised.

75 *against*: In preparation for.

77 *I have heard it over*: When Philostrate heard the play
is not a matter that will bear enquiry.

83 *simpleness*: Simplicity, innocence.

85 *wretchedness*: The lowly in both social position and intellect.

91 *respect*: Consideration.

92 *Takes it in might, not merit*: The meaning is clearly
'takes the will for the deed'. Presumably *in might* means
'according to their capability'. The irregularity of
metre suggests the possibility of corruption.

93 *clerks*: Scholars.

96 *Make periods in the midst of sentences*: As Prologue is
to do, 108–17.

104 *simplicity*: Sincerity, artlessness.

105 *to my capacity*: As far as I can understand, in my
opinion.

106 *addressed*: Ready.

107 *Flourish of trumpets*: This stage direction is not in Q.

It comes from F, and probably represents the stage practice of Shakespeare's company.

108 *If we offend* . . .: Presumably Quince reads from a scroll. The comic device by which a bad reader reverses the sense of what he is reading occurs in an earlier play, Nicholas Udall's *Ralph Roister Doister* (c. 1553, III.4). Quince's prologue is not in either *eight and six* or *eight and eight* (see III.1.22–4). Its form is that of a sonnet without the first four lines. Shakespeare uses the sonnet form for his prologue (or chorus) to *Romeo and Juliet* (Acts I and II).

116, 126 *show*: This may refer simply to the appearance of the characters in the play; but it is quite likely that they should adopt attitudes or even perform a mime, in the fashion of a dumb-show, suggestive of what is to come.

118 *stand upon*: Bother about.

points: Both 'trifles' and 'marks of punctuation'.

119 *rid*: Both 'rid himself of' and 'ridden'.

120 *stop*: In horsemanship, a sudden check in a horse's career; also the mark of punctuation.

123 *government*: Control.

125 *a trumpeter*: The trumpeter is mentioned in F, not in Q. He probably appeared in performances given by Shakespeare's company.

138 *hight*: Is called (an old-fashioned word in Shakespeare's time).

141 *fall*: Drop.

143 *tall*: Brave.

150 *At large*: At length.

152 *asses*: A subtly chosen word.

153 *interlude*: Play.

161 *right and sinister*: Right and left; horizontal.

161–2 *sinister . . . whisper*: The inexactness of the rhyme is of course part of the parody. An actor has been known to show Snout realizing the fault, and confusedly pronouncing 'whipister'. The effect was amusing. Shakespeare regularly accents *sinister* on the second syllable.

164 *wittiest*: Most intelligent.

partition: Wall *and* section of a speech or 'discourse'.

179 *sensible*: Capable of sensation.

180 *again*: Back, in return.

183 *pat*: Precisely.

189–90 *see a voice . . . spy an I can hear my Thisbe's face*: Another example of the comic dislocation of the senses.

190 *an*: If.

192 *thy lover's grace*: Thy gracious lover.

193–4 *Limander . . . Helen*: Presumably *Limander* is a mistake for 'Leander', Hero's lover; possibly it is influenced by Alexander, another name for Paris, lover of Helen of Troy.

195 *Shafalus . . . Procrus*: Mispronunciations of 'Cephalus' and 'Procris', a legendary pair of tragic lovers whose story is told in Ovid's *Metamorphoses*, Book VII. An English poem about them, by Thomas Edwards, was in existence by 1593 and survives in an edition of 1595.

200 *Tide life, tide death*: Come life, come death.

203 *mural down*: Wall down. A conjectural emendation (by Pope) of a difficult passage. See Collation 3 in An Account of the Text.

208 *in this kind*: That is, actors.

215–22 *You, ladies . . . life*: This passage (anticipated at I.2.70–78 and III.1.25–42) has provoked comparisons with an account of a happening at the Scottish Court on 30 August 1594. King James and his queen were celebrating the baptism of their son, Prince Henry, when a triumphal car was drawn into the hall by a blackamoor. 'This chariot should have been drawn in by a lion, but because his presence might have brought some fear to the nearest, or that the sight of the lights and torches might have commoved his tameness, it was thought meet that the Moor should supply that room' (from John Nichols's *Progresses of Elizabeth*, III.365). This is an interesting parallel with Shakespeare's play, though not necessarily an influence upon it.

220 *fell*: Fierce (also 'skin').

233 *lanthorn*: A variant form of 'lantern', preserved here for the sake of the pun.

234 *He should have worn the horns on his head*: A waggish remark at Moonshine's expense; horns were the mark of the cuckold.

235 *crescent*: A waxing moon.

242 *for the candle*: For fear of the candle.

243 *in snuff*: 'In need of snuffing' and 'in a rage'.

250–52 *All that I have to say . . . my dog*: Moonshine, in exasperation, lapses into prose.

255 *This is old Ninny's tomb*: Indicating a change of scene. No further indication is necessary, though directors have been known to employ a tomb inscribed *Hic iacet Ninus*. Thisbe gets the name wrong again (cf. III.1.90–91).

266 *beams*: So Q and F; often emended to 'gleams', both to avoid the repeated rhyming word, and to fit the alliterative scheme. But *beams* may be a deliberate comic touch.

270 *dole*: Cause of grief.

277 *Fates*: The three Fates in Greek mythology were Clotho, who carried a distaff, Lachesis, who wove the web of a man's life, and Atropos, whose shears cut the thread when the web was complete.

278 *Cut thread and thrum*: *Thread* is the warp in weaving; *thrum* the tufted end of the warp. *Thread and thrum* means 'good and bad together'; 'everything'. The image is ingeniously related both to the fates and to Bottom's trade.

279 *Quail*: Overpower.
    quell: Kill.

280 *passion*: Both 'suffering' and 'violent speech'.

286 *cheer*: Face.

299 *die*: One of a pair of dice.
    ace: A single spot on a die. *ace* was near enough in pronunciation to 'ass' to justify the pun in 303.

307 *passion*: Formal, or passionate, speech.

310 *mote*: In early editions *moth*, a common spelling for *mote*.

311–12 *he for a man . . . God bless us*: This was omitted from F, presumably because of a statute of James I forbidding profanity on the stage.

315 *means*: To 'mean' was both a dialect word meaning to 'lament' and a legal term meaning to 'lodge a formal complaint'. The legal term *videlicet* ('you may see') may suggest that both senses are felt here.

320 *tomb*: At this date, a true rhyme with 'dumb'.

322–7 *These lily lips . . . green as leeks*: The parodic derangement of epithets here recalls the confusions of the senses in earlier scenes.

328 *sisters three*: The Fates. This passage resembles the prologue to Thomas Preston's *Cambyses* (1569), a play of the kind that Shakespeare is burlesquing here:

> But he when sisters three had wrought to shear his
>   vital thread
> As heir due to take up the crown Cambyses did
>   proceed.

332 *shore*: That is, 'shorn' – a comic misuse for the sake of rhyme.

335 *Come, trusty sword*: In a comedy of 1607 called *The Fleire*, by Edward Sharpham, occurs the following passage:

> KNIGHT And how lives he with 'em?
> FLEIRE Faith, like Thisbe in the play, 'a has almost
>   killed himself with the scabbard.

This appears to record a piece of comic business in early performances of the play.

336 *imbrue*: Pierce; stain with blood.

342 *BOTTOM*: This speech is given to Bottom in F, but to Lion (that is, Snug) in Q. Shakespeare may have intended Snug to speak it.

343–4 *see the epilogue, or to hear a Bergomask dance*: A last touch of Bottom's characteristic verbal confusion.

344 *Bergomask*: A rustic dance after the manner of Bergamo, in Italy.

352 *A dance*: No distinct exeunt for the mechanicals is provided in the early editions. They obviously should

leave after the dance, before Theseus' reference to
their *palpable-gross play*.

356 *overwatched*: Stayed up late.

357 *palpable-gross*: Obviously crude.

360 *Enter Puck*: Puck's entry is often made through a trap-
door.

362 *behowls*: The original texts read *beholds*. The notion of
wolves howling against the moon was proverbial; cf.
As You Like It (V.2.104–5): ''tis like the howling of
Irish wolves against the moon'.

363 *heavy*: Weary.

364 *foredone*: Exhausted.

365 *wasted*: Used-up, burnt-out.

371 *Every one lets forth his*: Each grave lets forth its.

374 *triple Hecate*: The goddess Hecate ruled as Luna and
Cynthia in heaven, as Diana on earth, and as
Proserpine and Hecate in hell. Puck refers to her as
goddess of the moon and night.

377 *frolic*: Frolicsome, merry.

379–80 *I am sent with broom before . . . door*: Robin Goodfellow
traditionally had the duty of keeping the house clean,
and was often represented with a broom.

387 *rehearse . . . by rote*: Repeat from memory.

390 *Song and dance*: Some editors believe that the song has
been lost, with perhaps a separate *ditty* referred to in
385. Granville-Barker introduced 'Roses, their sharp
spines being gone' from *The Two Noble Kinsmen*. The
lines beginning *Now until the break of day* are headed
Ob. in Q1. F gives no speech-prefix, prints the lines in
italics and heads them *The song*. It is possible that these
lines were sung, perhaps by Oberon, with a chorus of
fairies. But there are objections. The lines are not
particularly lyrical: Oberon is giving a set of instruc-
tions. Also Shakespeare tends to differentiate his lyrics
by writing them in a metre different from what comes
before and after, whereas this is the same.

402 *mark prodigious*: Ominous, portentous birthmark.

405 *consecrate*: Consecrated, blessed.

406 *take his gait*: Take his way.

407 *several*: Separate.

413–28 *If we shadows have offended . . . amends*: These lines
form an epilogue, addressed directly to the audience.

418 *No more yielding but*: Yielding no more than.

423 *serpent's tongue*: Hisses (from the audience).

427 *hands*: That is, in applause.

The National: three theatres and so much more…
www.nationaltheatre.org.uk

In its three theatres on London's South Bank, the National presents an eclectic mix of new plays and classics, with seven or eight shows in repertory at any one time.

And there's more. Step inside and enjoy free exhibitions, backstage tours, talks and readings, a great theatre bookshop and plenty of places to eat and drink.

Sign-up as an e-member at www.nationaltheatre.org.uk/join and we'll keep you up-to-date with everything that's going on.

 NATIONAL THEATRE
SOUTH BANK
LONDON SE1 9PX

PENGUIN SHAKESPEARE

THE WINTER'S TALE
WILLIAM SHAKESPEARE

WWW.PENGUINSHAKESPEARE.COM

The jealous King of Sicily becomes convinced that his wife is carrying the child of his best friend. Imprisoned and put on trial, the Queen collapses when the King refuses to accept the divine confirmation of her innocence. The child is abandoned to die on the coast of Bohemia. But when she is found and raised by a shepherd, it seems redemption may be possible.

This book includes a general introduction to Shakespeare's life and the Elizabethan theatre, a separate introduction to *The Winter's Tale*, a chronology of his works, suggestions for further reading, an essay discussing performance options on both stage and screen by Paul Edmondson, and a commentary.

Edited by Ernest Schanzer

With an introduction by Russ McDonald

General Editor: Stanley Wells

PENGUIN SHAKESPEARE

TWELFTH NIGHT
WILLIAM SHAKESPEARE

WWW.PENGUINSHAKESPEARE.COM

Separated from her twin brother Sebastian after a shipwreck, Viola disguises herself as a boy to serve the Duke of Illyria. Wooing a countess on his behalf, she is stunned to find herself the object of his beloved's affections. With the arrival of Viola's brother, and a trick played upon the countess's steward, confusion reigns in this romantic comedy of mistaken identity.

This book includes a general introduction to Shakespeare's life and the Elizabethan theatre, a separate introduction to *Twelfth Night*, a chronology of his works, suggestions for further reading, an essay discussing performance options on both stage and screen, and a commentary.

Edited by M. M. Mahood

With an introduction by Michael Dobson

General Editor: Stanley Wells

PENGUIN SHAKESPEARE

CYMBELINE
WILLIAM SHAKESPEARE

WWW.PENGUINSHAKESPEARE.COM

The King of Britain, enraged by his daughter's disobedience in
marrying against his wishes, banishes his new son-in-law. Having fled
to Rome, the exiled husband makes a foolish wager with a villain he
encounters there – gambling on the fidelity of his abandoned wife.
Combining courtly menace and horror, comedy and melodrama,
Cymbeline is a moving depiction of two young lovers driven apart by
deceit and self-doubt.

This book includes a general introduction to Shakespeare's life and the
Elizabethan theatre, a separate introduction to *Cymbeline*, a chronology
of his works, suggestions for further reading, an essay discussing
performance options on both stage and screen, and a commentary.

Edited with an introduction by John Pitcher

General Editor: Stanley Wells

PENGUIN SHAKESPEARE

MUCH ADO ABOUT NOTHING
WILLIAM SHAKESPEARE

WWW.PENGUINSHAKESPEARE.COM

A vivacious woman and a high-spirited man both claim that they are
determined never to marry. But when their friends trick them into
believing that each harbours secret feelings for the other, they begin to
question whether their witty banter and sharp-tongued repartee
conceals something deeper. Schemes abound, misunderstandings
proliferate and matches are eventually made in this sparkling and
irresistible comedy.

This book includes a general introduction to Shakespeare's life and the
Elizabethan theatre, a separate introduction to *Much Ado About
Nothing*, a chronology of his works, suggestions for further reading, an
essay discussing performance options on both stage and screen, and a
commentary.

Edited by R. A. Foakes

With an introduction by Janette Dillon

General Editor: Stanley Wells

PENGUIN SHAKESPEARE

ALL'S WELL THAT ENDS WELL
WILLIAM SHAKESPEARE

WWW.PENGUINSHAKESPEARE.COM

A poor physician's daughter cures the King of France, and in return is promised the hand of any nobleman she wishes. But the man she chooses, the proud young Count of Rosillion, refuses to consummate the forced marriage and flees to Florence. Depicting the triumph of trickery over youthful arrogance, *All's Well that Ends Well* is among Shakespeare's darkest romantic comedies, yet it remains a powerful tribute to the strength of love.

This book includes a general introduction to Shakespeare's life and the Elizabethan theatre, a separate introduction to *All's Well That Ends Well*, a chronology of his works, suggestions for further reading, an essay discussing performance options on both stage and screen, and a commentary.

Edited by Barbara Everett

With an introduction by Janette Dillon

General Editor: Stanley Wells
